# THE DEHYDRATOR COOKBOOK
# FOR OUTDOOR ADVENTURERS

# THE DEHYDRATOR COOKBOOK

## FOR OUTDOOR ADVENTURERS

### HEALTHY, DELICIOUS RECIPES FOR BACKPACKING AND BEYOND

**Julie Mosier**

Photography by Darren Muir

ROCKRIDGE PRESS

*In memory of my mother, Denise,
and mother-in-law, Diana,
two remarkable women
both in and out of the kitchen.*

Interior and Cover Designer: Jami Spittler
Art Manager: Sue Bischofberger
Editor: Vanessa Ta
Production Manager: Riley Hoffman
Production Editor: Melissa Edeburn

Photography © 2019 Darren Muir

Author Photo: Henry Mosier

ISBN: Print 978-1-64152-579-4 | eBook 978-1-64152-580-0

# CONTENTS

# INTRODUCTION

About five years ago I took my first backpacking trip as an adult. I had grown up camping and backpacking with my parents but somehow didn't manage to get back out on the trail until I was in my forties. That first trip was a revelation to me. On that overnighter with just my dog for company, I learned how much I love the solitude of being in the backcountry and meeting the challenges of the trail. I took two important ideas away from that trip: One, I couldn't wait to go out and do it again, and two, I needed better food. The store-bought meals I had brought simply didn't live up to the rest of the experience. I decided to make my own meals for backpacking, and that meant learning how to dehydrate food.

So, I borrowed a dehydrator and started experimenting. My first step was to review cookbooks available at the time in order to understand the basic principles of dehydration. I started simply, dehydrating pastas, ground meat, and vegetables. Then I began to add prepared mixes and dehydrated powders, but I quickly learned that type of meal didn't interest me. I tried dehydrating some complete meals, such as a bean chili, and Pasta with Sausage and Braised Peppers—a recipe that I still make and have included in this book (page 120). These meals definitely had more texture and flavor than the premade meals I was able to buy at the time. Experimenting with dehydrated meals soon expanded beyond simply feeding myself while out on the trail—I began to feed these foods to friends and family as well. I learned how to develop recipes that would stretch the boundaries of my newly acquired skills. I tried dehydrating braised beef and pork and even learned how to dehydrate salads that could be rehydrated in cold water.

Though I learned how to dehydrate food in order to create backcountry meals, I've discovered many other ways dehydrated food can be useful. For example, dehydrated food is a great substitute for airline food—the Black Bean and Corn Couscous Salad (page 100) can be rehydrated in cool water and makes a refreshing meal midflight. Dehydrated meals can be carried in an RV or camper pantry or stashed in the panniers of a motorcycle for cross-country trips. The White Bean Chicken Stew with Grilled Poblanos (page 112) makes a satisfying meal on the road, and the Coconut Rice Pudding with Golden Raisins (page 151) is a great way to end (or start) the day.

I also encourage you to think outside the box. Dehydrated food has uses beyond making great meals for travelers. These meals are a wonderful addition to your home pantry. For example, you can have a healthy, fresh-tasting dinner such as Spicy Sweet Potato and Chorizo Stew (page 106) on days when you don't feel like cooking or you didn't make it to the grocery store. Dehydrating your own meals ensures that you can have the flavors you love available to you all the time.

Dehydrating foods is also a great way to save money. Stock up on foods when they are in season and available at a lower price and dehydrate them for future use. Or, better yet, preserve the harvest from your garden using some of the recipes in this book. Maybe your garden is bursting with tomatoes and zucchini at the end of the summer. Both vegetables dry very well and can be rehydrated and added to soups, salsas, or pasta salads.

You can minimize food waste by dehydrating ingredients or even making full meals with foods that are approaching their expiration date. If you have fruits or veggies in your refrigerator that will expire before you can use them, cut them up and stick them in the dehydrator to preserve them for future use. Perhaps you found a great deal on broccoli at the store and bought more than you can eat right away: Take advantage of the dehydrator by making some Savory Broccoli Bites (page 143). The recipes in this book will give you a great starting place for how to prepare meals for your outdoor adventures, as well as making the most of your pantry and garden or farmers' market finds.

I'll walk you through everything you need to know in order to create your own healthy dehydrated meals, including how to find the right dehydrator, the tools and equipment you'll need, how best to store dehydrated foods, and how to prepare them out on the trail. Keep in mind that this collection of recipes for dehydrated fruits, vegetables, legumes, seafood, and meats is only the beginning. Once you've mastered the basics of dehydration, you'll be able to adapt the techniques described on these pages to create your own favorite dehydrated meals, giving you more time on your adventures to enjoy the scenery and the experience.

Let's get started!

PART ONE

# BASICS OF DEHYDRATING FOR THE OUTDOORS

Food is an integral part of any outdoor adventure. The longer and more difficult the outing, the more important the food becomes. Whether you are just starting to explore the backcountry and are uncertain about what food to take with you, or you are a thru-hiker with food fatigue and a need to mix it up, making your own food for the trail is a great way to ensure that your meals match your needs and enhance your experience.

Dehydration is an ideal method of preserving food for the outdoor adventurer; it's an easy process, and removing most of the moisture from food makes it lightweight—your back will thank you! For example, you can use your dehydrator to make snacks to take on the trail with you, such as Vegetable Bean Salsa (page 145) to be eaten with tortillas. Or you can dehydrate soups and stews such as Porter-Infused Chili with Bacon (page 109) to sustain you on energy-crushing hikes.

In this section, I'll walk you through the first steps of dehydration, from selecting a dehydrator to preparing, packing, and storing dehydrated food.

# CHAPTER ONE

# DEHYDRATING 101

First things first. If you are totally new to dehydrating, after reading this chapter, take a look in your cabinets to see what equipment you already have, then make a list of what you'll need to buy. The main piece of equipment used in all the recipes is a dehydrator. There are numerous models on the market, appropriate for any budget. Another option is an oven. If your oven can go as low as 170°F and has air circulation, you can use it to dehydrate certain foods.

# The Right Dehydrator

There are many dehydrators on the market, and selecting the best one to fit your needs can feel overwhelming. Models come with a wide range of features and vary considerably in price, with basic dehydrators costing around $40 and top-end models costing $500 or more. So, how do you find the model that's right for you?

The first step is to think about how you might use the dehydrator. Many different foods can be dehydrated, including fruits and vegetables, grains and legumes, and meats and seafood. You can dehydrate complete meals. You can also dehydrate herbs and flowers, and even make yogurt. All the recipes in this book can be made successfully using any dehydrator on the market.

In the next section I'll break down the available types of dehydrators and their features and provide information to help you decide which model to buy. If you already own a dehydrator, keep reading: This section includes info and tips to better understand your dehydrator.

## Round or Box Dehydrator?

Dehydrators are available in round or box models. This section will walk you through how dehydrators work and the differences between the two types.

Round dehydrators circulate air vertically and typically have the motor and fan at the bottom of the unit. They have a lower price point and typically have a bit less drying room than a box dehydrator. The dehydration trays stack on top of each other, and a lid covers the unit. Round dehydrators usually come with four to six trays. Some models offer the option to buy additional trays, allowing you to increase the available square footage of drying room. Make sure the model has a screen covering the fan, to prevent bits of food debris from falling into the motor. Food on trays closer to the bottom of the dehydrator may dry faster than food on trays at the top, and you'll have to monitor this, removing food as it dries and rotating trays to ensure even drying. The dehydrator that you choose also needs to be powerful enough to dry your food—600 watts is sufficient for five or more trays.

Box dehydrators circulate air horizontally, with a motor and fan at the back of the dehydrator that pushes air past all the trays. Box dehydrators usually start at around $150 but can be much more expensive. These models typically have more drying room than a round dehydrator, but you cannot increase the number of trays. Box units usually have between seven and eleven trays. Look for a dehydrator that has a fan diameter of at least five inches, but the larger diameter the better because a larger fan pushes air more evenly throughout the unit. To make sure all your food dries evenly, you may have to rotate the trays 180 degrees on their rack or move trays up and down within the unit. This will ensure that air circulates across all the food. The amount of circulation will depend not only on the fan size but also the amount and type of food in the dehydrator. Box dehydrators tend to be a bit noisier than round dehydrators and also have a larger footprint, so take that into consideration when making your selection.

# TOP FIVE DEHYDRATORS

The following dehydrators are great options in a range of different price points.

**Presto 06301 Dehydro Digital Electric Food Dehydrator.** This is a basic round dehydrator with a compact footprint. It comes with 5 shelves and is expandable to 12 shelves, with a temperature range of 90°F to 165°F. This model is a great choice for those just learning how to dehydrate food. $59.

**NESCO FD-1018A Gardenmaster Food Dehydrator.** This round dehydrator comes with 8 trays and expands up to 30 trays. At 1000 watts, it has plenty of power to dry that many trays. Temperatures range from 95°F to 160°F. The dehydrator comes with several tray accessories. This is a great option for larger families or people with a bountiful garden harvest to preserve. $108.

**Cabela's 10-Tray Deluxe Dehydrator.** This is a sturdy box dehydrator from a reliable brand. It has a temperature range of 80°F to 165°F and good air circulation. This dehydrator is available at a low price for a box dehydrator, and it is a workhorse that can be used day after day. $150.

**Excalibur 3926TW 9-Tray Electric Food Dehydrator.** Excalibur has been making dehydrators for decades and is considered to be a high-quality manufacturer. This box model has both a timer and programmable heat. It has nine slide-in trays providing 15 square feet of drying space. The flexible trays allow for making soups and fruit leathers without worry of run off. $295.

**TSM D-10 Dehydrator.** Both the housing and shelves are stainless steel. This box dehydrator comes with 10 shelves, an 800-watt motor, and a temperature range of 90°F to 165°F. Several tray accessories are available. Stainless steel is a very durable, dishwasher-safe material. $620.

# Key Features

Dehydrator models offer many different features. Here are several features to consider:

**Accessories.** Reusable sheets to cover the mesh on the trays are essential for making fruit leather or dishes with more liquid, such as stews and soups. Some dehydrators offer jerky-making supplies. Look for accessories that are packaged with the dehydrator or buy additional accessories later. Most accessories will work in multiple brands of dehydrators.

**Capacity.** Round dehydrator trays provide about 1 square foot of drying space per tray, or about a cup and a half of food, and box dehydrators provide around 1.3 square feet per tray, or about two cups of food.

**Footprint.** Consider how much counter space you have for your dehydrator and where you will store it when it is not in use.

**Noise.** Dehydrators can be noisy. If you find your dehydrator is too noisy for comfort, you may want to set it up in your garage (if you have one) or time the drying to run overnight or during periods when you'll be out of the house.

**On/Off Switch.** This seems like a basic option, but some dehydrators lack an on/off switch, requiring you to plug it in and unplug it to turn it on and off.

**Temperature Settings.** Avoid dehydrators that don't allow you to select a temperature—not all foods dehydrate at the same temperature.

**Timer.** This feature allows you to set the dehydrator for a specific amount of time. This is also a safety feature in case you are not available when the dehydrator's cycle is complete. If your dehydrator does not have a timer, you can buy an appliance timer, plug your dehydrator into it, and set the timer for the number of hours needed. It will shut off automatically when the timer goes off.

**Wattage.** Look for 450 to 600 watts in a round dehydrator, and 600 watts if you plan to purchase and use additional trays. Look for a minimum of 600 watts in a box dehydrator to ensure your food dries evenly and in an efficient amount of time.

# Principles of Dehydrating

Dehydrators perform a simple operation: A fan and motor circulate heated air through the machine, which results in the removal of moisture from the food on the dehydrator trays. Foods with high water content, such as bell peppers, take longer to dehydrate than foods with a lower water content, such as kale. Likewise, food with a high density, such as a large bean, will take longer to dry than food with a lower density, such as rice.

To get the best results when dehydrating the recipes in this book, pay close attention to the directions for prepping the vegetables. If the recipe calls for cutting the vegetables into ½-inch dice, be sure to cut them to that size so they will dehydrate at the same rate as the rest of the recipe. If you are uncertain what ½-inch dice looks like, measure and cut a piece to that size and set it aside as a guide. Cutting larger pieces than is called for is easy to do by accident, and that will affect how the recipe itself turns out, the drying time, and the consistency of the food.

When food comes out of the dehydrator, it looks vastly different from its original state. Hummus and soups can look as cracked and parched as a desert floor. Food can come off the trays in thin sheets, which you can break into smaller pieces. Properly dried pieces of fruit bend but don't break, and they do not feel moist when you squeeze them. Other foods— vegetables, grains, and legumes— should be hard and dry.

It is possible to burn food in a dehydrator, so pay attention to both the temperature and timing recommendations given in the recipes. Also, when you're learning how to dehydrate food, be sure to check the food every few hours. You may need to rotate the trays to ensure that the food dries evenly, and if you find that part of your recipe is dry before the rest, remove that part and store it while the rest of the recipe continues to dry. There is often one ingredient in each recipe that takes longer to dry than the rest, and that ingredient will be called out in the recipe as the barometer for when the food is dry. In the Red Curry Vegetable Stir-Fry (page 134), for example, that ingredient is the red bell pepper, which has a very high water content.

The amount of food that will fit on a dehydrator tray varies somewhat, based on viscosity or density, so some experimentation will be required. Start with about one cup of food and spread it out evenly, to about ½ inch from the edge of the tray. You should have an even, thin layer of food, with no significantly larger chunks. If there is still room on the tray once the food is spread out, you can add a bit more until the entire tray surface is full.

## DRYING FOOD

Dehydration is a simple and ancient means of preserving food. Drying food was a way to save and store harvests of fruit, grains, and vegetables. Laying out food on mats to dry under the sun morphed into hand-built dehydrator boxes with mesh trays. Once ovens with reliably consistent temperatures existed, food was dried on oven trays. Some people still use ovens for dehydration, and if your oven has a minimum temperature setting of lower than 170°F and convection air, you may be able to use it for dehydrating food. Now we have the convenience of electric dehydrators that offer several improvements over other methods. Different types of foods require specific temperatures for food safety and the most efficient drying times. Circulating air prompts faster drying times as well.

# Essential Tools and Equipment

Dehydration is mostly about prep work, so having the appropriate tools will make your job easier. Make sure you have the following tools on hand.

**Baking sheet.** If you don't already have one, a good-quality baking sheet that disperses heat properly and doesn't buckle under high heat is a great addition to your kitchen. Use it for roasting vegetables and fish.

**Blender.** Blenders are great for making purées for sauces, soups, and fruit leather. A food processor or immersion blender also works for this purpose.

**Four-cup measuring pitcher.** These pitchers are good for measuring liquids and for measuring the yield of dehydrated foods (if you don't have a kitchen scale).

**Kitchen knife.** Aside from the dehydrator itself, a kitchen knife is the most important tool for dehydrating. A good knife will make your prep work much easier. Perhaps you already have a favorite knife—one that keeps a good edge, has a straight blade, and is comfortable to hold for extended periods. Good knives don't need to be expensive. In our kitchen we use the same knives many culinary schools offer; they are inexpensive but great tools for the job.

**Kitchen scale.** An inexpensive digital scale is very useful for measuring ingredients with precision and is also helpful for measuring and portioning the completed and dehydrated meals.

**Parchment paper.** Line baking sheets with parchment paper to prevent food from sticking to the pan. It also makes for easy cleanup.

## Bonus Items

These items are by no means necessary, but they are nice to have (and they all have uses far beyond dehydration).

**Mandoline.** This is an excellent tool for making precise and consistent slices. Consistency is a key factor in proper dehydration, and if you need a veggie to be cut to a ¼-inch thickness, a mandoline is an easy way to ensure that consistency.

**Vacuum sealer.** This is an excellent gadget for preparing your dehydrated food for long-term storage. A vacuum sealer removes most of the oxygen from the stored food, which prolongs its shelf life.

### CLEANING YOUR DEHYDRATOR

Be sure to clean your dehydrator between uses to avoid cross contamination and transference of odors. To clean the dehydrator, wipe down the housing inside and out with hot, soapy water and wash all the trays and accessories. The tray shape can make it a bit awkward to run them through a dishwasher, but a quick hand wash with hot, soapy water will do the trick. If your trays do fit on the bottom rack of your dishwasher, be sure to check the dehydrator manual to ensure the trays will withstand the heat of the lower rack.

If you have a box dehydrator, check the back of the unit occasionally to make sure that the screen covering the fan and motor is free of dust and debris. If you have a round dehydrator, pull all the trays out to look at the base and ensure that all debris has been cleared from the area surrounding the fan and motor.

# Storage

Proper storage is essential to lengthening the shelf life of your dehydrated food. Air, moisture, heat, and light all contribute to the degradation of dehydrated foods. Once your food is dehydrated, open the lid of the dehydrator and let the food cool to room temperature before storing it. Cooling the food first will prevent condensation from developing inside the storage containers.

Storage containers should be airtight and kept out of the light if the containers are not opaque, and in a climate-controlled space, for example your pantry rather than your garage. You can use glass jars or zip-sealed storage bags. Select a container that can be labeled with a marker or some tape. If possible, store the food in trail-friendly containers, such as boil-in bags. Boil-in bags come in many sizes; a 5-by-8-inch bag will fit a single serving of all the recipes in this book. These are food-safe, thick plastic bags with a zip seal. The recipes in this book that require boiling water to rehydrate the food call for boil-in bags. Please note that it is important to select bags specifically made to hold boiling water, otherwise they will not stand up to the heat and will melt. For dishes that are rehydrated using cold water, a regular gallon-size zip-sealed bag works just fine. For these cold-soak recipes, simply add cool water directly to the bag to rehydrate your meal.

## Dividing the Recipes

Most of the recipes in this book make complete meals, so once the food is dehydrated, you have the choice of either storing the entire amount in one container or portioning the meal into individual servings. Whichever method you choose, you'll want to measure the full amount made and calculate the measurement of each portion based on the specified quantity of servings.

This is where a kitchen scale comes in handy. For example, say you determine that the full recipe weighs 24 ounces. There are 4 servings in the recipe, so each serving should be 6 ounces. If you don't have a kitchen scale, you can use a large measuring pitcher to calculate the volume of each serving. If the full batch is 3 cups, and the recipe is for 4 servings, then each serving will be ¾ of a cup.

Be sure to label your containers with the name of the meal, the date the meal was made, the expiry date, and the amount of water needed to rehydrate each serving.

Carefully distribute the types of food evenly into trail bags. There's nothing worse than getting a bag that's mostly noodle and very little sauce, and realizing there's another bag at home that's all sauce and hardly any noodles. Break longer ingredients such as linguine into smaller pieces either when it goes into the pot to cook, or if you forget, on the tray after drying it. You can press your flat hand on the noodles to break them up before bagging them; it is much easier to load the bags when the pieces are less than 3 inches long.

# Shelf Life

Dehydrated food is shelf stable for months, sometimes up to a year, depending on the type of food and the storage conditions. In recipes containing different food types, I have applied the shortest expiration of an ingredient to the entire recipe. That is to say, if the recipe contains veggies that are stable for 6 months and meat that is only stable for 2 months, the entire meal will be labeled as stable for 2 months.

Generally speaking, meats can be stored for up to 2 months, or 6 months if in vacuum-sealed bags in the freezer. Fruits and vegetables can be safely stored for a year under the proper conditions, and most grains can be stored for at least a year. If you are making food for your outdoor adventures, use your food within the same season in which it was made for the best flavor and greatest nutritional value.

# CHAPTER TWO

# PREPARING FOR YOUR ADVENTURE

Here comes the fun part—the planning! Pore over those maps to determine your route and possible campsites along the way, lay out your gear, and take test runs with your equipment. And, of course, part of the planning process is deciding what food you will bring, how you will pack it, and the best way to prepare it once you're on the trail. Knowing what equipment to bring for preparing your food and how to use it will make mealtimes much more enjoyable. This chapter provides some tips on both how to plan your menu and how to pack the food for your adventure.

# Planning Meals

Some of us love the planning process and see it as part of the overall enjoyment of the trip. For others, it's a necessary chore. Whichever way you view it, your trip will go more smoothly with proper planning. These tips will make that process easier for you.

To make a meal plan, start by counting the number of meals needed. Going for a weekend adventure? Plan for a snack and dinner for Friday night and a full day's meals for Saturday. For Sunday you'll need breakfast and a snack. To ensure that you don't run out of food, it's a good idea to carry a small amount of extra food. For a short trip you might want to pack one extra meal and an additional two snacks. This way you can maintain your energy if the trip takes a bit longer than you expected or your needs are higher than anticipated thanks to exertion or chilly weather. For a longer trip, consider taking about 10 percent more food than you anticipate needing. For a five-night trip, take enough meals for one more full day. Once you have a few trips under your belt, you will be better able to gauge your food needs.

## Stick with What You Know

Your first backpacking trip is not the time to experiment with unfamiliar flavors, so choose foods that you already know and like. Do you eat oatmeal at home? Take that on the trail. The Cinnamon Apple Hazelnut Oatmeal (page 71) makes a hearty breakfast to start your day. Don't worry about having a different breakfast each day unless you plan to be out for several days; it's much easier to prepare a larger batch of a single meal than it is to prepare multiple recipes. Do you like sandwiches for lunch? Plan to take the ingredients for a wrap such as the Roasted Vegetable and Hummus Wrap (page 117). Wraps are easy to prepare on the trail while you're taking a break for lunch. Plan for a warm dinner at the end of the day—you'll appreciate the reward after putting in the miles. A hearty stew or casserole such as Spicy Sweet Potato and Chorizo Stew (page 106) might be just the ticket.

Don't forget about snacks! They will sustain you between meals and offer some variety along the trail. Plan for three or four snacks per day, depending on the number of miles you are hiking and the time between meals. Snacks should be easy to eat while hiking, so divide them into individual portions for easy access from your pack. A large handful per portion is a great place to start. Again, go with your favorite foods: For me it's nuts and dried fruits, some salty mixes such as pretzels or sesame sticks with roasted pumpkin seeds, and maybe a bit of chocolate.

## DO A TEST RUN

**Just as you would test your gear, do a test run on preparing your food at home. Make sure you know how to light your stove, that you have a way to measure water, and that you know what properly rehydrated food looks and tastes like. The trip itself is an adventure, so be sure to dial in your food to give you the freedom to enjoy the trail!**

# Sample Menu: Two-Night Trip

## FRIDAY AFTERNOON (BEGINNING TRIP)

Snack: Crispy Chickpeas

Snack: Savory Broccoli Bites

Dinner: Porter-Infused Chili with Bacon

## SATURDAY

Breakfast: Cinnamon Apple Hazelnut Oatmeal,
Coconut Chai

Snack: Hummus and Tortillas

Lunch: Black Bean and Corn Couscous Salad

Snack: Salmon Jerky

Snack: Savory Broccoli Bites

Dinner: Cilantro Pesto Pasta with Veggies

Dessert: Coconut Rice Pudding with
Golden Raisins

## SUNDAY (COMING OFF THE TRAIL)

Breakfast: Cinnamon Apple Hazelnut Oatmeal,
Coffee/Tea

Snack: Crispy Chickpeas

Snack: Fruit Leather

# What to Pack

Remember, hiking with a pack burns a lot of energy, and your body needs proper fueling to maintain its strength and endurance. Extra calories will be needed to keep you warm on chilly nights as well.

So, how much food should you plan to pack? If you are already very active in your daily life, you may know your caloric needs, but if not, consider adding 20 to 40 percent more calories than you eat in a typical day. Adjust this amount up or down a bit based on the number of miles you plan to hike each day. As a general rule, when you are carrying a pack, you're burning about 120 calories per mile. If it's a shorter trip, say between five and seven miles per day, then adding 30 percent more calories should be enough. If you have a more strenuous trip planned, say you will be hiking between 10 and 15 miles per day, then lean toward adding 40 percent more calories. Once you get into the realm of doing a thru-hike, everything changes and you can't pack enough calories. Many thru-hikers end up walking between 20 and 35 miles per day, depending on the elevation profile. In this case, you will want to load up on as much food as possible.

## By Calorie Breakdown

Breaking down the calories you should aim to consume for each snack or meal based on the length of your trip can help you determine how much food to pack. Here are a few examples:

- ➤ **For a shorter mileage trip,** if you typically eat 2,000 calories per day, pack around 2,600 calories per full day—about 600 calories each for breakfast and lunch, 650 for dinner, and four snacks of 200 calories each.

- ➤ **For longer trips,** if you typically eat 2,000 calories per day, pack around 3,000 calories per full day—about 650 calories each for breakfast and lunch, 800 for dinner, and several snacks of 200 calories each.

- ➤ **For thru-hikes,** if you typically eat 2,000 calories per day, pack between 3,500 and 4,000 calories per day—about 800 calories each for breakfast and lunch, 1,000 calories for dinner, and a few snacks of 400 calories each.

# Getting Organized

Once you've selected the meals and snacks that you'll be taking, it's time to pack them in an organized way so the food takes up as little space as possible. Start with a list of what you'll be eating and how many servings of each meal or snack you plan to take. Don't forget to list what you plan to drink in addition to water, and any seasonings or condiments you'll want with your meals.

Once you have your list, gather the foods. If you've stored your dehydrated meals in single-serving bags, as suggested on page 12, gathering your meals will be simple. If your foods are stored in bulk, now is the time to portion them out. Snacks can either be stored in bulk bags, with handfuls taken out as you need them, or stored in individual serving sizes in small zip-sealed bags. I mix the two methods. I learned this lesson from experience: There are a few snacks that I'm likely to plow through on the first day if I haven't divided them into single servings!

## Modular Packing

There are several ways to organize your food in your pack. I'm a modular packer, so all the items in my pack are grouped by similarity of function and stored in a bag. I use different colored dry bags or stuff sacks to help me quickly identify the contents of each bag within my pack. For example, my kitchen bag is red, and I pack everything I need to make and eat a meal inside it. With this color-coded system, I can find exactly what I need as soon as I open my pack.

I put all the different colored bags into my pack in the order in which I intend to take them out. I keep the food bag at the top of the pack for easy access when I stop for lunch or snacks. I also stick a few snacks in my hip pad pocket on my backpack so I can easily access them while I'm on the move.

# What to Know about Cooking on the Trail

By creating complete dehydrated meals using the recipes in this book, such as Cilantro Pesto Pasta with Veggies (page 125), you're able to pack the meal into individual servings before leaving home. Then when you're on the trail, all you'll need to do is bring some water to a boil to rehydrate your meal. In a few cases you can even use cool water to rehydrate a salad for lunch.

## Cookware

Since most of the cooking happens in your kitchen, you won't need too many cooking items on the trail. Keep it simple and you'll have less to carry. Here are the basic necessities:

**Bowl and cup.** If you plan to eat all your meals out of the bag, you won't need a bowl, but most people like to have a container for eating and drinking. For many, this is the same container; others prefer to have both a bowl and a cup. There are collapsible and nesting models that offer you compact, lightweight options. Your cup can also be used to measure the amount of water needed for rehydrating your meals.

**Eating utensil.** Most people use a spork—a combination of a fork and spoon—to cut down on the number of utensils they have to carry. There are plastic sporks, which are inexpensive but tend to break, and there are titanium sporks, which are more expensive but durable. Both options are very lightweight. If you plan to eat your meals directly out of the bag, consider getting a long-handled spoon so you can reach the food in the bottom of the bag without having to stick your whole hand into the bag.

**Garbage bag.** A gallon-size zip-sealed bag can be used to store all your waste. Alternatively, you can turn the zip-sealed bags left over from your first few meals into garbage bags. Everything you bring in needs to be packed out, whether it's food waste or packaging.

**Insulated lunch bag.** These are optional but handy. Using an insulated bag shortens the rehydration time of your meals and is particularly helpful on chilly nights when it can keep the food hot during the rehydration process. Choose a bag that folds down when not in use, so it doesn't take up much room, or plan to store items in the bag when it's packed in your backpack. Alternatively, you can use your jacket for insulation, wrapping it around the meal bag while it's rehydrating. *Important: Do not use your jacket as insulation if you are in bear country; adding food odors to your clothing may attract bears.*

**Stove and fuel.** There are several stove types on the market. See the next section for more details about picking the perfect stove.

## Stoves

The most important component of your trail kitchen is the stove. There are several different types on the market. Although it's great to have options, too many choices can be overwhelming if you're buying a stove for the first time, so here is some information to help you make the best choice.

**Canister stoves are probably the most commonly used stoves these days.** Canister stoves have a burner, gas regulator, and a device to support the pot. The stove often screws directly to the fuel source, whereas other stoves have fuel line connections. Canister stoves are lightweight, easy to set up and use, and they heat water and food quickly and efficiently. Some models come with an integrated canister—a water canister that attaches to the heating unit, providing better heat transfer and some wind protection. These models are designed mainly for heating water. Other models may have a small platform to accommodate a separate pan. Canister stoves run on an isobutane-propane fuel that is purchased in nonrefillable containers. The fuel is a bit more expensive than other types. Keep in mind that canister stoves don't work as well in very cold weather.

Canister stoves start at $25 with more expensive models costing $150. Jetboil is the most common integrated canister stove. The smallest integrated canister stove is a great size for a single person, whereas the 1.5-liter size is a better choice for families. The Jetboil stoves start at $80 and run up to $150.

**Liquid fuel stoves are also popular options for backcountry campers.** Compared with canister stoves, liquid fuel stoves are more complicated to use and require that the fuel bottle be pressurized and the burner primed before each use. Liquid fuel stoves also tend to be a bit heavier than canister stoves. The fuel type most commonly used in these stoves is white gas, which may be easier to find outside the United States. The fuel bottles are refillable. The liquid fuel stove tends to work better than a canister stove in cold weather and works well for larger groups, as the fuel is less expensive. Liquid fuel stoves start at $100 and the fuel bottles cost around $20. MSR Whisperlite is the most common brand and model.

**Alternative fuel stoves tend to have one thing in common across the numerous available varieties:** They are slower to heat up than either a canister or liquid fuel stove. Each type of alternative fuel stove has advantages and disadvantages. Wood-burning stoves, for example, don't require you to pack fuel, which means you carry less weight, but you do have to find fuel at your campsite, and some areas ban wood-burning stoves. Denatured alcohol stoves are very lightweight but don't burn as hot, so you need more fuel. Generally, alternative fuel stoves require windbreaks.

Regardless of which stove you select, be aware that there is inherent risk in igniting any stove in a backcountry environment. Read the directions for your stove carefully, and practice setting up and lighting the stove at home before taking it on a trip.

If you are primarily heating water to rehydrate your meals, which is the case with all the recipes in this book, an integrated canister stove may be your best bet. If you do purchase an integrated canister stove, you won't need to bring along an additional pot. But if you have a liquid fuel stove, an alternative fuel stove, or a canister stove that is not integrated, you will need a lightweight pot that holds at least three cups of water. For a pot that's both lightweight and durable, look for hard-anodized aluminum or titanium. Hard-anodized aluminum pots start at $30, and a titanium cookpot will cost around $35.

# Cooking Dehydrated Foods

The recipes in part 3 of this book detail how to make complete dehydrated meals. Since no cooking is required on the trail beyond heating water to rehydrate the food, mealtime on the trail is super easy. Dehydrated meals reduce the amount of equipment you need to carry and the time you need to spend preparing food. In the end you're left with great-tasting meals and more time to enjoy the scenery.

By and large, rehydrating food is just a matter of pouring the correct amount of water over the food, mixing it well, insulating it to quicken the rehydration time, and waiting between 10 and 20 minutes for your meal to be ready. It's really that simple. Each recipe in this book lists the amount of water needed for rehydration and the average time it will take to rehydrate your meal. Keep in mind that ambient temperature will affect the timing of rehydration, and insulating the meal will speed up the process.

Most meals will take 1 cup of water or less to rehydrate. The soups and stews will take a little more. A few recipes call for some toppings to be added to your meal; for example, the Sesame Ginger Kale Slaw (page 95) recipe calls for some crunchy sliced almonds to be sprinkled over your meal after it's rehydrated.

One thing to consider is where you would like to eat. If you are planning on having a cold-soak salad for lunch, you may want to pull the salad out of your pack 15 minutes ahead of the time you want to eat, add the water to rehydrate it, mix it up, stick it back in your pack, and walk a little farther until you find somewhere picturesque to eat lunch.

You'll find some designated cold-soak recipes in this book. These recipes are designed to rehydrate in the same amount of time as a hot meal—about 15 minutes—but offer you the convenience of not stopping to take out your stove and heat water. Keep in mind, too, that any meal can be cold soaked if you have the time to wait for it. Meals that call for hot water might take up to an hour to rehydrate when using cold water, but using cold water is an option for people who want to minimize the equipment they take and the weight they carry. In fact, going stoveless is becoming a more popular choice. If you decide to try leaving the stove at home, simply plan enough time for your meals to rehydrate, and always insulate the meal bag to hasten the rehydration time.

## CONSIDER THE SCENT

**If your meal includes foods with strong odors, such as salmon or tuna, consider eating your meal somewhere other than your campsite in order to avoid attracting unwanted visitors. Also, if you know that you will be traveling through bear country, plan to pack only foods with minimal odor and do not eat at your campsite.**

PART TWO

# DEHYDRATING FOOD AT HOME

Learning how to dehydrate foods is a great way to save money and extend your food budget, preserve excess harvest from the garden, and even reduce food waste by drying fruit or vegetables that may be nearing their expiration date. This chapter walks you through the basics of dehydrating individual foods such as apples and pears, sweet potatoes, and carrots, and grains and legumes such as rice and lentils. Once you have the basics down, you'll see how easy it is to incorporate dehydrating into your kitchen routine.

# CHAPTER THREE

# FRUITS AND VEGETABLES

If you've never dehydrated food before, this chapter will help ground you in the basics. Once you've mastered dehydrating fruits, vegetables, and legumes/grains, you should be very comfortable with your dehydrator, making the rest of the recipes in this book a snap to produce. Before long, you will be on the trail, eating tasty and nutritious home-cooked meals. Each section in this chapter provides instructions for dehydrating a few foods, although those same methods can be applied to most foods in that particular category, unless otherwise noted. Once you've tried dehydrating apples and pears, for example, you can apply the same methods to stone fruits such as peaches and plums.

# Fruit

For many people, dried fruit may be their first introduction to dehydrated food. Who hasn't bought some dried apple slices to snack on while on the trail? Drying fruit is quite simple, and it's the perfect way to get to know your dehydrator. Many different fruits can be dehydrated, and, with a shelf life of 6 months or longer, simple dried fruit is a tasty snack to make in batches and store for hiking season.

## APPLES AND PEARS

**PREP TIME:** 15 minutes

**YIELD:** 1 apple or pear yields about ½ cup dried fruit; this recipe makes 2 cups

*Dried apples and pears make great snacks on their own, or you can chop them up and add them to a nut mix for a combination of savory and sweet flavors. Choose ripe apples of your favorite variety, and pears that are ripe but not mushy.*

4 apples or pears, peeled and cored
2 tablespoons freshly squeezed lemon juice, optional
3 cups water, optional

### To Prepare

1. Slice each fruit into ¼-inch slices, either crosswise or lengthwise.

2. If desired, you can dip the slices into a solution of 2 tablespoons of lemon juice and 3 cups of water to slow down the browning of the fruit flesh, but it's not necessary. Doing so will not affect the flavor of the fruit.

CONTINUED ➤

### To Dehydrate

1. Place the fruit slices on the dehydrator trays, leaving a little space between the slices.

2. Place the trays in the dehydrator. Set the dehydrator to 125°F and turn it on. If your dehydrator has a built-in timer, set it for 4 hours. For models without a timer, set a separate timer.

3. At the 4-hour mark, check the fruit. It's done when it will bend but not break and isn't moist to the touch. If necessary, continue to dry the fruit for another 1 to 2 hours. Feel free to taste a piece at any point; you are looking for a slightly chewy texture.

### To Store

Once the fruit is dried and has cooled to room temperature, place it in an airtight container such as a zip-sealed bag with the excess air pushed out, a vacuum-sealed bag, or a jar with a tight-fitting lid. Store the container out of the light and away from heat for up to 6 months.

# KIWI

**PREP TIME:** 10 minutes

**YIELD:** 5 kiwis yields about 1 cup dried fruit; this recipe makes 2 cups

*Slices of dried kiwi are an awesome snack when you need a bit of sweetness. Look for kiwis that are firm but not hard and avoid fruits with mushy spots.*

**10 kiwis, peeled**

## To Prepare

1. Cut off the stem end of each peeled kiwi.

2. Slice the kiwis into generous ¼-inch rounds.

## To Dehydrate

1. Place the kiwi slices on the dehydrator trays, leaving a little space between the slices.

2. Place the trays in the dehydrator. Set the dehydrator to 125°F and turn it on. If your dehydrator has a built-in timer, set it for 6 hours. For models without a timer, set a separate timer.

3. At the 6-hour mark, check the fruit. It's done when it bends but doesn't break and isn't moist to the touch. If necessary, continue to dry the fruit for another 1 to 2 hours. Taste a piece at any point; you're looking for a slightly chewy texture.

## To Store

Once the fruit is dried and has cooled to room temperature, place it in an airtight container such as a zip-sealed bag with the excess air pushed out, a vacuum-sealed bag, or a jar with a tight-fitting lid. Store the container out of the light and away from heat for up to 6 months.

# STRAWBERRIES AND BLUEBERRIES

**PREP TIME:** 15 minutes

**YIELD:** 1 pint strawberries yields ¾ cup dried fruit; 1½ cups blueberries yields ⅔ cup dried fruit

*All berries can be dried, but some work better than others. The size, structure, and moisture content of strawberries make them a perfect choice. Blueberries can be dried but will take more time to dry than other berries. Raspberries are more challenging to dry than strawberries because of their higher water content and softer structure.*

---

**2 pints strawberries, stems removed**

**or**

**4½ cups blueberries**

---

## To Prepare

1. Wash the berries thoroughly and pat them dry.

2. Slice the strawberries into ¼-inch slices.

3. Gently smash the blueberries, breaking the skin and slightly flattening them.

### To Dehydrate

1.  Place the berries on the dehydrator trays, leaving a little space between the berries.

2.  Place the trays in the dehydrator. Set the dehydrator to 125°F and turn it on. If your dehydrator has a built-in timer, set it for 6 hours. For models without a timer, set a separate timer.

3.  At the 6-hour mark, check the fruit. It's done when it looks wrinkled, it bends but doesn't break, and it isn't moist to the touch. If necessary, continue to dry the berries for another 1 to 2 hours.

### To Store

Once the fruit is dried and has cooled to room temperature, place it in an airtight container such as a zip-sealed bag with the excess air pushed out, a vacuum-sealed bag, or a jar with a tight-fitting lid. Store the container out of the light and away from heat for up to 6 months.

# FRUIT LEATHER

**PREP TIME:** 15 minutes

**YIELD:** 1 tray of leather makes 2 rolls

*Making fruit leather is easy, and it's a great way to use fruit that may be past its prime. The combinations of fruit blends are endless. The one factor to consider when deciding which fruits to include is the amount of pectin in the fruit. A certain amount of pectin is required for the fruit to set into leather. Apples have plenty of natural pectin, so a great solution is to include some applesauce in whatever flavor combination sounds good to you. Remember that both flavor and sweetness will intensify when the fruit is dried, so don't add sugar to the mix. Here is one of my favorite flavor combinations.*

½ cup unsweetened applesauce
½ cup blueberries

## To Prepare

1. Wash the blueberries and pat them dry.

2. Put the applesauce and blueberries in a blender and purée them until they are very smooth.

## To Dehydrate

1. When drying foods such as fruit purée, it's essential to use a solid insert for the mesh dehydrator tray to ensure that no liquid drips through the tray. Pour the purée onto a dehydrator tray fitted with a solid plastic insert. Spread the purée evenly so that there are no thin spots or mounds. This will help the fruit dry evenly.

2. Place the trays in the dehydrator. Set the dehydrator to 125°F and turn it on. If your dehydrator has a built-in timer, set it for 3 hours. For models without a timer, set a separate timer.

3. At the 3-hour mark, check the leather. It's done when the leather is no longer sticky to touch and the leather can be pulled off the tray in a sheet. Do not let the leather get so dry that it turns brittle.

## To Store

Pull the leather off the tray and place it on a cutting board. Cut the leather into lengths 4 to 5 inches wide and roll them up. Place the rolls in an airtight container such as a zip-sealed bag with the excess air pushed out, a vacuum-sealed bag, or a jar with a tight-fitting lid. Store the container out of the light and away from heat for up to 1 year.

# Vegetables

Drying vegetables is a good way to minimize food waste or preserve an overabundant crop from your garden. Dehydrated vegetables can be stored and added to pasta dishes or soups when you want a little extra color or flavor in your meal. Although most vegetables can be dehydrated, the drying time will vary depending on the amount of water in the fresh vegetable. Tomatoes and red peppers will take more time than green beans or broccoli, for example. The drying time of water-heavy vegetables can be reduced by cutting them into smaller pieces and making sure they aren't too thick—a ¼-inch slice is a good thickness for the dehydrator.

# ROOT VEGETABLES AND TUBERS

**PREP TIME:** 10 to 20 minutes

**YIELD:** Varies by vegetable, but about one-third of the fresh vegetable

*4 cups sliced carrots, turnips, parsnips, sweet potatoes, or yucca can be dehydrated with ease. White potatoes do not dehydrate as well.*

## To Prepare

1. Wash and peel the vegetables.

2. Cut the vegetables into pieces just under ¼ inch thick and 1 to 2 inches long.

## To Dehydrate

1. Arrange the vegetable pieces on the dehydrator trays, leaving a little space between the pieces.

2. Place the trays in the dehydrator. Set the dehydrator to 130°F and turn it on. If your dehydrator has a built-in timer, set it for 6 hours. For models without a timer, set a separate timer.

3. At the 6-hour mark, check the vegetables. They should be stiff and dry and not moist to the touch. The vegetables should not bend easily.

## To Store

Once the vegetables are dried and have cooled to room temperature, store the slices in an airtight container such as a zip-sealed bag with the excess air pushed out, a vacuum-sealed bag, or a jar with a tight-fitting lid. Store the container out of the light and away from heat for up to 1 year.

# TOMATOES

**PREP TIME:** 15 minutes

**YIELD:** 1 cup cherry tomatoes yields about ⅓ cup dried

*Dried tomatoes can be used in many dishes or eaten on their own as a snack. Small cherry tomatoes make a great sweet-tart snack. They are water-heavy so cut them into pieces to reduce the drying time.*

---

**3 cups cherry tomatoes**

---

## To Prepare

1. Wash and dry the tomatoes.

2. Cut smaller cherry tomatoes in half and cut larger ones into quarters.

## To Dehydrate

1. Place the tomato pieces skin-side down on a solid tray insert. (Due to their high sugar content, the tomatoes will stick to the mesh trays if you don't use the solid insert, so although the insert isn't absolutely necessary, using it does make cleanup much easier.)

2. Place the trays in the dehydrator. Set the dehydrator to 130°F and turn it on. If your dehydrator has a built-in timer, set it for 8 hours. For models without a timer, set a separate timer.

3. At the 8-hour mark, check the tomatoes. They should be pliable but not moist. They should not squish when pinched.

**To Store**

Once the vegetables are dried and have cooled to room temperature, store the slices in an airtight container such as a zip-sealed bag with the excess air pushed out, a vacuum-sealed bag, or a jar with a tight-fitting lid. Store the container out of the light and away from heat for up to 1 year.

# MUSHROOMS, RED BELL PEPPER, EGGPLANT, ZUCCHINI, ONIONS

**PREP TIME:** 10 to 20 minutes

**YIELD:** Varies by vegetable, but about one-quarter of the fresh vegetable

*Vegetables that have a higher water content and can be sliced are easy to dehydrate. Dried mushrooms, red bell pepper, eggplant, zucchini, and onions make great additions to soups and stews.*

---

**4 cups sliced mushrooms, red bell pepper, eggplant, zucchini, or onions**

---

## To Prepare

1. Wash and dry the vegetables.

2. Cut the vegetables into pieces no more than ¼ inch thick and 2 to 3 inches long. Cut and core bell peppers, removing the seeds and stems. For onions, remove the papery skin and separate the onion layers. For zucchini, slice them so there is a bit of skin on each piece—otherwise the pieces will fall apart when they are rehydrated. Eggplant should be peeled and can be either sliced or cut into ½-inch cubes.

**To Dehydrate**

1. Arrange the vegetables on the dehydrator trays, leaving a little space between the pieces.

2. Place the trays in the dehydrator. Set the dehydrator to 130°F and turn it on. If your dehydrator has a built-in timer, set it for 7 hours. For models without a timer, set a separate timer.

3. At the 7-hour mark, check the vegetables. They should be stiff and dry and not moist to the touch. The pieces should not bend easily.

**To Store**

Once the vegetables are dried and have cooled to room temperature, store the slices in an airtight container such as a zip-sealed bag with the excess air pushed out, a vacuum-sealed bag, or a jar with a tight-fitting lid. Store the container out of the light and away from heat for up to 1 year.

# CHAPTER FOUR

# GRAINS AND LEGUMES

Grains and legumes are ideal nutritional choices for the trail. Both quinoa and lentils are high in protein, and nearly all grains and legumes rehydrate well. Many grains and legumes can be added to a soup or stew recipe to increase the calorie and protein content of your meal. Grains and legumes can also be added to rehydrated vegetables for a simple meal. Dehydrating grains and legumes such as rice, barley, millet, quinoa, beans, split peas, and lentils is a straightforward process.

# GENERAL RECIPE

**PREP TIME:** 35 minutes

**YIELD:** Varies by grain and legume

---

**1 cup rice, barley, millet, quinoa,
beans, split peas, or lentils**

---

## To Prepare

1. Cook the grain or legume according to the package directions until fully cooked. Consider using broth instead of plain water to add a bit more flavor. You don't want the grains or legumes to have a mushy consistency when cooked, but you do want to cook them a minute or two beyond al dente.

2. Drain the grains or legumes and rinse if the package directions recommend doing so.

## To Dehydrate

1. Spread out the grains or legumes evenly on dehydrator trays fitted with a solid plastic insert or sheet.

2. Set the dehydrator to 130°F and turn it on. If your dehydrator has a built-in timer, set it for 4 hours. For models without a timer, set a separate timer.

3. Place the trays in the dehydrator. At the 4-hour mark, check the grains or legumes. They're done when they are hard to the touch. If necessary, continue to dry them for another 1 to 2 hours.

CONTINUED ➢

## To Store

Once the grains or legumes are dried and have cooled to room temperature, store them in an airtight container such as a zip-sealed bag with the excess air pushed out, a vacuum-sealed bag, or a jar with a tight-fitting lid. Store the container out of the light and away from heat for up to 1 year.

## To Rehydrate

Some grains can be cold-water rehydrated, such as the lentils in the Lemony Lentil Salad (page 97), or white rice and quinoa. Other grains, such as farro or brown rice, need hot water and a bit more time to fully rehydrate.

# COUSCOUS

**PREP TIME:** 15 minutes    **COOK TIME:** 5 minutes

**YIELD:** 2 cups

*Couscous cooks so quickly that it does not need to be cooked and dehydrated unless you want to cook the couscous with broth or water flavored with spices and herbs. If you plan to cook couscous in plain water, you can simply boil water on the trail, add the couscous, take the water off the heat, cover the pot, and let it sit for five minutes. If you want to add some flavor to your couscous, prepare it at home and dehydrate it according to the directions here. Try a couple tablespoons of chopped cilantro and a small squeeze of lime juice, or a teaspoon of crushed lemongrass or ginger root.*

1½ cups broth or water
½ teaspoon olive oil
½ teaspoon salt (if using water)
1 cup couscous
Flavoring (optional, see headnote)

**To Prepare**

1. Bring the water, oil, and salt (if using), to a boil.

2. Add the couscous and flavoring (if using). Remove from the heat, stir, cover, and let sit for 5 minutes. Fluff the couscous with a fork.

CONTINUED >

**To Dehydrate**

1. Spread out the couscous evenly on the dehydrator trays fitted with a solid plastic insert or sheet.

2. Place the trays in the dehydrator. Set the dehydrator to 135°F and turn it on. If your dehydrator has a built-in timer, set it for 4 hours. For models without a timer, set a separate timer.

3. At the 4-hour mark, check the couscous. It should be firm and not moist to the touch. If necessary, continue to dry the couscous for another 1 to 2 hours.

**To Store**

Once the couscous is dried and has cooled to room temperature, store it in an airtight container such as a zip-sealed bag with the excess air pushed out, a vacuum-sealed bag, or a jar with a tight-fitting lid. Store the container out of the light and away from heat for up to 1 year.

# RICE PILAF

**PREP TIME:** 15 minutes   **COOK TIME:** 30 minutes

**YIELD:** 3 cups cooked rice

*Rice can be boiled or baked, and a wide variety of flavorings can be added during the cooking process. Baking rice is a great way to impart flavor. A simple rice pilaf will add flavor to any meal.*

---

1 teaspoon oil

¼ cup finely diced onion (¼-inch dice)

1 teaspoon minced garlic

1 cup rice

¼ teaspoon salt

2 cups water or broth

---

**To Prepare**

1. Preheat the oven to 350°F.

2. Heat the oil in a saucepan over medium heat. Add the onion and cook for 2 minutes, stirring occasionally. Add the garlic and cook for an additional 30 seconds.

3. Add the rice to the pan and cook for 4 to 5 minutes, stirring occasionally, until the rice starts to turn opaque and slightly golden.

4. Remove the rice from the heat and pour it into a 9-inch square baking pan. Add the salt and water, stir to combine, and cover the baking dish with aluminum foil. Bake for 30 minutes.

CONTINUED ➤

### To Dehydrate

1. Spread out the baked rice evenly on dehydrator trays fitted with a solid plastic insert or sheet.

2. Place the trays in the dehydrator. Set the dehydrator to 135°F and turn it on. If your dehydrator has a built-in timer, set it for 4 hours. For models without a timer, set a separate timer.

3. At the 4-hour mark, check the rice. It should be firm and not moist to the touch. If necessary, continue to dry the rice for another her 1 to 2 hours.

### To Store

Once the rice is dried and has cooled to room temperature, store it in an airtight container such as a zip-sealed bag with the excess air pushed out, a vacuum-sealed bag, or a jar with a tight-fitting lid. Store the container out of the light and away from heat for up to 1 year.

> **Tip:** The rice pilaf can be livened up by adding a tablespoon of chopped herbs, or switching the garlic for another aromatic such as ginger.

CHAPTER FIVE

# MEAT AND SEAFOOD

Most people have eaten jerky as a snack on the trail at some point. It's a great source of both protein and sodium for high-activity days. Jerky is also easy to pack and carry. Beyond jerky, most kinds of meat and some fish can be dehydrated, but some special care in preparation is needed to ensure that the meat will also rehydrate well. It's important to keep in mind that rehydrated meat will have a different texture than fresh meat, and some meats will retain a chewy characteristic regardless of preparation or rehydration time. Meats that are cooked more slowly—braised, for example—will respond better to rehydration than meats that are cooked rapidly, such as when stir-fried.

Chicken is best when cooked slowly, and it will take longer to rehydrate than other meats. Chicken cooked in a pressure cooker will rehydrate a bit more easily. If you don't have a pressure cooker, you can buy canned chicken that has been pressure cooked.

Meat has a higher fat content than grains and vegetables. Because of the fat content, home-dehydrated meat should only be stored for a few months; any longer and the fat may go rancid, so keep this in mind when prepping. Choose lean meats and trim all visible fat prior to cooking. Drain as much fat from the meat as possible after cooking, blotting and squeezing the meat with paper towels to remove the fat. While meat or fish is dehydrating, check the trays occasionally and blot any surface oil with a paper towel.

# BEEF JERKY IN TWO FLAVORS

**PREP TIME:** 45 minutes    **MARINATING TIME:** 4 to 12 hours
**DEHYDRATION TIME:** 5 to 7 hours    **YIELD:** 2 cups

*Jerky is a great way to get protein on the trail and makes a tasty snack to munch on while walking. These recipes will get you started if it's your first time making jerky. The apple and bourbon impart a subtle flavor to the beef, and the sesame and ginger give it a bold flavor profile.*

### Apple Bourbon Beef Jerky

1½ pounds flank steak

1¼ cups apple juice

3 tablespoons dark brown sugar

3 tablespoons bourbon

1 teaspoon salt

¾ teaspoon freshly ground
   black pepper

¾ teaspoon onion powder

¼ teaspoon ground cinnamon

### Sesame Ginger Beef Jerky

1½ pounds flank steak

½ cup soy sauce or tamari

½ cup water

¼ cup agave or honey

2 teaspoons minced garlic

2 teaspoons minced ginger

1 teaspoon toasted sesame oil

3 scallions, cut in 2-inch lengths

**To Prepare**

1. Place the flank steak in the freezer for 30 to 40 minutes to firm up slightly. This will make slicing it easier.

2. In a small bowl, mix together all the other ingredients for the marinade of your choice.

CONTINUED ➤

3. Trim the steak of all visible fat. If the steak is thicker than ⅓ inch, slice it in half lengthwise, then slice it into 1-inch strips across the grain. You should end up with strips that are 1 inch wide and ¼ inch thick.

4. Combine the steak strips with the marinade in a gallon-size zip-sealed bag, and gently knead the bag to mix the beef with the marinade. Chill the bag in the refrigerator for 4 to 12 hours.

5. Remove the steak from the bag and discard the marinade.

## To Dehydrate

1. Arrange the strips of steak on mesh dehydrator trays, leaving a little space between each strip.

2. Place the trays in the dehydrator. Set the dehydrator to 160°F and turn it on. If your dehydrator has a built-in timer, set it for 2 hours and 30 minutes. For models without a timer, set a separate timer.

3. At the 2½-hour mark, turn the strips over, using a paper towel to blot any oil on the surface of the meat. Reset the timer for another 2 hours and 30 minutes. The jerky is ready when it can bend but not break apart and does not feel moist. If necessary, continue to dry the jerky for another 1 to 2 hours.

## To Store

Homemade jerky can be stored for up to 2 months in a zip-sealed bag in the refrigerator, or for up to 4 months in a vacuum-sealed bag in the freezer.

# GROUND TURKEY JERKY

**PREP TIME:** 20 minutes    **MARINATING TIME:** 30 minutes to 2 hours
**DEHYDRATION TIME:** 4 to 6 hours    **BAKING TIME:** 10 minutes    **YIELD:** 1½ cups

*Ground meat is a great option for making jerky. Buy the best quality meat you can for great flavored jerky, and be sure to chill the meat mixture before spreading it out to cut into strips.*

---

**Zest and juice of 1 lemon**

**1 tablespoon agave**

**1 tablespoon Worcestershire sauce**

**2 teaspoons apple cider vinegar**

**1 garlic clove, minced**

**1 teaspoon salt**

**1 teaspoon freshly ground black pepper**

**½ teaspoon dried thyme**

**1 pound ground turkey, at least 93 percent lean**

---

## To Prepare

1. In a medium bowl, combine the lemon zest and juice, agave, Worcestershire sauce, vinegar, garlic, salt, pepper, and thyme and stir well to mix. Add the turkey to the bowl and knead the mixture with your hands until all the ingredients are thoroughly combined. Cover the bowl and chill the mixture in the refrigerator for 30 minutes to 2 hours.

CONTINUED ➤

2. Remove the bowl from the refrigerator, turn out the turkey mixture onto a sheet of waxed or parchment paper, and flatten the mixture slightly. Cover with an additional piece of wax or parchment paper and flatten the turkey mixture with a rolling pin or your hands until the mixture is ½ inch thick.

3. Remove the top piece of paper and cut the turkey mixture into strips 1 inch wide and about 5 inches long.

### To Dehydrate

1. Arrange the strips of turkey mix onto mesh dehydrator trays, leaving a little space between each strip. (Wetting your knife or spatula and hands occasionally keeps the turkey from sticking as you transfer the strips.) Make sure that the strips are not stretched out too thinly, and fill in any holes so the strips maintain a ½-inch thickness.

2. Place the trays in the dehydrator. Set the dehydrator to 150°F and turn it on. If your dehydrator has a built-in timer, set it for 4 hours. For models without a timer, set a separate timer.

3. At the 4-hour mark, check the turkey strips. The jerky is ready when it can bend but not break apart and does not feel moist. If necessary, continue to dry the strips for another 1 to 2 hours.

4. Preheat the oven to 250°F. Place the strips on a baking sheet and bake for 10 minutes to ensure the meat is free of bacteria.

### To Store

Homemade jerky can be stored for up to 2 months in a zip-sealed bag in the refrigerator, or for up to 4 months in a vacuum-sealed bag in the freezer.

# SALMON JERKY

**PREP TIME:** 25 minutes    **MARINATING TIME:** 4 hours    **COOK TIME:** 10 minutes
**DEHYDRATION TIME:** 4 to 6 hours    **BAKING TIME:** 10 minutes    **YIELD:** 3 cups

*Salmon jerky is a delicious snack to eat on the trail, but keep in mind when planning your meals and snacks that foods with strong odors, such as salmon, can attract bears. If you are hiking in bear country, carefully choose where you will be eating your salmon jerky; also take care when disposing of the packaging. Enclose the packaging inside another zip-sealed bag and dispose of it in a trash can at the first opportunity. (That means don't sleep next to where you eat this jerky!)*

1 (1½-pound) salmon fillet
½ cup soy sauce or tamari
2 tablespoons brown sugar
½ teaspoon freshly ground black pepper
½ teaspoon smoked paprika
1 garlic clove, minced
1 tablespoon freshly squeezed lemon juice

## To Prepare

1. Freeze the salmon fillet for 30 minutes before cutting, for easier slicing.

2. Mix the soy sauce, sugar, pepper, paprika, garlic, and lemon juice in a small bowl.

3. Remove any pin bones from the salmon and slice it into ¼-inch strips.

CONTINUED ⊳

4. Combine the salmon strips and marinade in a gallon-size zip-sealed bag and gently knead to mix the salmon with the marinade. Chill the bag in the refrigerator for 4 hours.

5. Preheat the oven to 250°F. Remove the salmon from the bag and discard the marinade. Place the salmon strips on a baking sheet and bake for 10 minutes. This brings the internal temperature of the salmon to 160°F for safety. A digital thermometer is handy for checking the internal temperature of the salmon.

## To Dehydrate

1. Place the salmon strips on mesh dehydrator trays, leaving a little space between each strip.

2. Place the trays in the dehydrator. Set the dehydrator to 160°F and turn it on. If your dehydrator has a built-in timer, set it for 4 hours. For models without a timer, set a separate timer.

3. Periodically check the salmon, and if necessary, use a paper towel to absorb any oil from the surface of the salmon.

4. At the 4-hour mark, check the salmon. Salmon will dehydrate more quickly than red meat. The salmon is ready when it can bend but not break, and it should be slightly chewy, not crispy. If necessary, continue to dry the salmon for another 1 to 2 hours, checking often for doneness.

## To Store

Homemade jerky can be stored for up to 2 months in a zip-sealed bag in the refrigerator, or for up to 4 months in a vacuum-sealed bag in the freezer.

# PART THREE

# RECIPES FOR YOUR ADVENTURES

And finally, the recipes! If you jumped straight to this section, be sure to read part 1 to benefit from all the trip tips and recommendations to get the most out of these recipes. Each recipe in this section is a complete meal that you can enjoy out on the trail. Best of all, you'll do the bulk of the work in your own kitchen as you prepare these tasty, nutritious meals for your backcountry adventures.

When looking over the recipes, refer to chapter 2 for hints on planning meals for your trip. Once you are on the trail, you can simply rehydrate the meals with hot water (or in some cases cold water) and appreciate the view while you enjoy your food.

Note: All the following recipes have labels letting you know if they're free from dairy, gluten, meat, nuts, soy, and sugar, and if the recipe is suitable for vegans. Even if the recipe is designated gluten-free, it's important to check the ingredient labels on all gluten-free products to ensure they were processed in a completely gluten-free environment.

CHAPTER SIX

# BREAKFAST

Whether you are a morning person or not, the recipes in this chapter are a great way to start your day. Protein counts range from 11 grams all the way up to 38 grams, giving you multiple options based on your planned miles for the day. If you'll need more calories during the morning than these recipes provide, try pairing your chosen dish with a Power Shake (page 89) for some extra energy first thing.

# FRUIT AND NUT COUSCOUS

**DAIRY FREE · GLUTEN FREE · SOY FREE · VEGAN**

**PREP TIME:** 15 MINUTES  **COOK TIME:** 5 MINUTES
**DEHYDRATION TIME:** 3 TO 5 HOURS  **REHYDRATION TIME:** 10 MINUTES
**WATER NEEDED FOR REHYDRATION (PER SERVING):** ¾ CUP

**SERVES:** 4

¾ cup water

¾ cup coconut milk

1 tablespoon agave

½ teaspoon salt

1 cup couscous

¾ cup dried peaches, diced (see page 31 for instructions on drying apples and pears)

½ cup dried blueberries (see page 34 for instructions on drying berries)

½ cup finely chopped skinned hazelnuts

*The coconut milk in this recipe gives the couscous a creaminess that's very comforting at breakfast. Try some different fruit and nut combos to mix it up.*

## To Prepare

1. In a medium pot, combine the water, coconut milk, agave, and salt. Bring the mixture to a boil.
2. Add the couscous, peaches, and blueberries to the pot, then remove the pot from the heat and stir the mixture. Cover the pot and set it aside for 5 minutes.
3. Fluff the couscous with a fork and stir in the hazelnuts.

## To Dehydrate

1. Spread the couscous mixture out evenly on the dehydrator trays fitted with a solid plastic tray insert.

CONTINUED >

2. Place the trays in the dehydrator. Set the dehydrator to 135°F and turn it on. If your dehydrator has a built-in timer, set it for 3 hours. For models without a timer, set a separate timer.

3. At the 3-hour mark, check the couscous. It should be firm and not feel moist. If necessary, continue to dry the couscous for another 1 to 2 hours.

**To Store**

Measure the total amount of couscous, divide it into four portions, and place each portion in a boil-in bag. Label and date the bags. Store for up to 9 months.

**To Rehydrate**

Add ¾ cup of boiling water to the bag. Mix it well, cover, and let it sit for about 10 minutes. Stir the couscous again before eating.

**NUTRITIONAL INFORMATION (PER SERVING)**: 450 calories, 18g fat, 66g carb, 10g protein, 310mg sodium (13% DV).

# CINNAMON APPLE HAZELNUT OATMEAL

**DAIRY FREE · GLUTEN FREE · SOY FREE · VEGAN**

**PREP TIME:** 20 MINUTES  **DEHYDRATION TIME:** 4 TO 6 HOURS  **REHYDRATION TIME:** 5 MINUTES
**WATER NEEDED FOR REHYDRATION (PER SERVING):** 1 CUP

**SERVES:** 4

2 cups gluten-free rolled oats (or regular oats if you tolerate gluten)

½ cup finely chopped, roasted hazelnuts

2 tablespoons hemp hearts

1 ½ tablespoons flaxseed meal

1 tablespoon packed brown sugar

¼ teaspoon salt

2 cups peeled and cored apples

½ teaspoon ground cinnamon

*Apples and cinnamon are a classic combination, and the hazelnuts add a crunchy twist to this energy-boosting oatmeal. It's easy to double this recipe, and it stores well for future trips.*

## To Prepare

1. In a medium bowl, mix together the oats, hazelnuts, hemp hearts, flaxseed meal, brown sugar, and salt. Set the bowl aside.
2. Cut the apples into slices ¼ inch thick and 1 inch wide.
3. In a small bowl, toss the apples with the cinnamon.

## To Dehydrate

1. Place the apple slices on the dehydrator trays, leaving a little space between the slices.
2. Place the trays in the dehydrator. Set the dehydrator to 135°F and turn it on. If your dehydrator has a built-in timer, set it for 4 hours. For models without a timer, set a separate timer.

CONTINUED ➤

3. At the 4-hour mark, check the apples. They should bend but not break and should not feel moist. If necessary, continue to dry the apples for another 1 to 2 hours.

**To Store**

Combine the oatmeal mix with the apples. Measure the total amount, divide it into four portions, and place each portion in a boil-in bag. Label and date the bags. Store for up to 12 months.

**To Rehydrate**

Add 1 cup of boiling water to the bag. Mix it well, cover, and let it sit for about 5 minutes. Stir the oatmeal again before eating.

**NUTRITIONAL INFORMATION (PER SERVING)**: 360 calories, 15g fat, 50g carb, 11g protein, 150mg sodium (6% DV).

## Preparation Tip

For a creamier oatmeal, add a tablespoon of milk powder or plant-based milk powder to each bag before adding the water.

# CARROT PINEAPPLE OATMEAL

**DAIRY FREE · GLUTEN FREE · SOY FREE · VEGAN**

**PREP TIME:** 20 MINUTES **DEHYDRATION TIME:** 4 TO 6 HOURS **REHYDRATION TIME:** 10 MINUTES
**WATER NEEDED FOR REHYDRATION (PER SERVING):** ¾ CUP

**SERVES:** 4

2 cups gluten-free rolled oats (or regular oats if you tolerate gluten)

¼ cup chopped walnuts

¼ cup packed golden raisins

2 tablespoons hemp hearts

1½ tablespoons flaxseed meal

¼ teaspoon salt

¾ cup matchstick carrots

⅓ cup finely chopped canned pineapple, plus 2 tablespoons pineapple juice

3 large dates, pitted and minced

½ teaspoon canola or other healthy oil

½ teaspoon vanilla extract

⅛ teaspoon ground cinnamon

*Carrot cake is a beloved and comforting dessert. This recipe pays tribute to those flavors in a sustaining oatmeal. The hemp hearts provide some extra protein for energy on the trail.*

## To Prepare

1. In a medium bowl, mix together the oats, walnuts, raisins, hemp hearts, flaxseed meal, and salt. Set the bowl aside.
2. In a small bowl, mix together the carrots, pineapple, pineapple juice, dates, oil, vanilla, and cinnamon.

## To Dehydrate

1. Spread the pineapple/carrot mix out evenly on the dehydrator trays fitted with a solid plastic tray insert.
2. Place the trays in the dehydrator. Set the dehydrator to 130°F and turn it on. If your dehydrator has a built-in timer, set it for 4 hours. For models without a timer, set a separate timer.

CONTINUED ➤

3. At the 4-hour mark, check the pineapple/carrot mix. It should be firm and should not feel moist. If necessary, continue to dry the mixture for another 1 to 2 hours.

**To Store**

Add the pineapple/carrot mix to the oatmeal mix. Measure the total amount, divide it into four portions, and place each portion in a boil-in bag. Label and date the bags. Store for up to 12 months.

**To Rehydrate**

Add ¾ cup of boiling water to the bag. Mix it well, cover, and let it sit for about 10 minutes. Stir the oatmeal again before eating.

**NUTRITIONAL INFORMATION (PER SERVING)**: 390 calories, 12g fat, 64g carb, 11g protein, 160mg sodium (7% DV).

**Tip**
This is an easy recipe to double and will store well for future trips.

# NUTTY COCONUT GRANOLA

**DAIRY FREE · GLUTEN FREE · SOY FREE · VEGAN**

**PREP TIME:** 20 MINUTES  **COOK TIME:** 1 HOUR TO 1 HOUR, 10 MINUTES
**DEHYDRATION TIME:** 4 TO 6 HOURS

**SERVES:** 8

3 cups gluten-free rolled oats (or regular oats if you tolerate gluten)

1 cup unsweetened coconut chips

1 cup sliced almonds

½ cup roasted salted pepitas (pumpkin kernels)

¼ cup loosely packed brown sugar

2 tablespoons hemp hearts

¼ teaspoon salt

¼ cup maple syrup

2 tablespoons coconut oil

1 cup diced dried mango (¼-inch dice) (see page 31 for instructions on drying apples and pears)

¼ cup minced crystallized ginger

*This granola recipe has a ton of flexibility. Swap out the mango and almonds for your favorite dried fruits and nuts to create a new flavor profile.*

## To Prepare

1. In a large bowl, mix the oats, coconut chips, almonds, pepitas, brown sugar, hemp hearts, and salt. Stir to combine.

2. Add the maple syrup and oil and stir to combine thoroughly.

## To Dehydrate

1. Spread the granola out evenly on the dehydrator trays fitted with a solid plastic tray insert.

2. Place the trays in the dehydrator. Set the dehydrator to 155°F and turn it on. If your dehydrator has a built-in timer, set it for 4 hours. For models without a timer, set a separate timer.

3. At the 4-hour mark, check the granola. It should be dry and slightly crisp and should not feel moist. If necessary, continue to dry the granola for another 1 to 2 hours.

CONTINUED ➤

### To Store

Measure the total amount of granola, divide it into eight portions, and place each portion in a zip-sealed bag. Label and date the bags. Store for up to 6 months.

### To Eat

Granola does not need to be rehydrated. It can be eaten dry or with the milk of your choice.

**NUTRITIONAL INFORMATION (PER SERVING)**: 460 calories, 21g fat, 51g carb, 11g protein, 125mg sodium (5% DV).

## Preparation Tip

1. You can also prepare granola in the oven. Preheat the oven to 250°F, and line a baking sheet with parchment paper.
2. Spread the granola out evenly on the prepared baking sheet, pressing down gently on the mix with your hands.
3. Bake for 60 to 70 minutes, stirring the granola a couple of times as it bakes.
4. When the granola has cooled add the mango and ginger pieces.

# HAZELNUT BERRY GRANOLA

**DAIRY FREE · GLUTEN FREE · SOY FREE · VEGAN**

**PREP TIME:** 20 MINUTES **COOK TIME:** 1 HOUR TO 1 HOUR, 10 MINUTES
**DEHYDRATION TIME:** 4 TO 6 HOURS

**SERVES:** 8

3 cups gluten-free rolled oats (or regular oats if you tolerate gluten)

⅓ cup unsweetened coconut chips

1½ cups chopped skinned hazelnuts

½ cup roasted salted pepitas (pumpkin seeds)

¼ cup loosely packed brown sugar

2 tablespoons hemp hearts

¼ teaspoon salt

⅓ cup agave

3 tablespoons coconut oil

½ cup dried blueberries (see page 34 for instructions on drying berries)

1 cup chopped dried strawberries (see page 34 for instructions on drying berries)

*Hazelnuts and berries are a classic Northwest combination. Try swapping the agave for maple syrup for a slightly different flavor.*

## To Prepare

1. In a large bowl, mix the oats, coconut chips, hazelnuts, pepitas, brown sugar, hemp hearts, and salt. Stir to combine.

2. Add the agave and oil to the bowl and stir to combine thoroughly.

## To Dehydrate

1. Spread the granola out evenly on dehydrator trays fitted with a solid plastic tray insert.

2. Place the trays in the dehydrator. Set the dehydrator to 155°F and turn it on. If your dehydrator has a built-in timer, set it for 4 hours. For models without a timer, set a separate timer.

3. At the 4-hour mark, check the granola. It should be dry and slightly crisp and should not feel moist. If necessary, continue to dry the granola for another 1 to 2 hours.

CONTINUED >

### To Store

Measure the total amount of granola, divide it into eight portions, and place each portion in a zip-sealed bag. Label and date the bags. Store for up to 6 months.

### To Eat

Granola does not need to be rehydrated. It can be eaten dry or with the milk of your choice.

**NUTRITIONAL INFORMATION (PER SERVING)**: 610 calories, 25g fat, 88g carb, 12g protein, 260mg sodium (11% DV).

## Preparation Tip

1. You can also prepare granola in the oven. Preheat the oven to 250°F and line a baking sheet with parchment paper.
2. Spread the granola out evenly on the prepared baking sheet, pressing down gently on the mix with your hands.
3. Bake for 60 to 70 minutes, stirring the granola a couple of times as it bakes.
4. When the granola has cooled, add the dried blueberries and strawberries.

# SALMON AND ROASTED SWEET POTATO HASH

**DAIRY FREE** • **NUT FREE** • **SOY FREE** • **SUGAR FREE**

**PREP TIME:** 30 MINUTES  **COOK TIME:** 30 MINUTES  **DEHYDRATION TIME:** 7 TO 9 HOURS
**REHYDRATION TIME:** 15 MINUTES  **WATER NEEDED TO REHYDRATE (PER SERVING):** ½ CUP
**SERVES:** 4

1½ pounds skinless
salmon fillet

1 teaspoon salt, plus more
for seasoning salmon

½ teaspoon freshly ground
black pepper, plus more for
seasoning salmon

Olive oil cooking spray

5 cups diced sweet potatoes
(¾-inch dice)

1 large onion, cut into
1-inch dice

1 large red bell pepper, cut
into 1-inch dice

¾ teaspoon smoked paprika

2 tablespoons coarsely
chopped fresh dill, or
2 teaspoons dried dill

¼ cup chopped flat
leaf parsley

*Salmon and sweet potatoes are a great pairing
in this breakfast hash, with the onion and bell
pepper adding a touch of sweetness. When meal
planning, remember that foods with strong
odors, such as salmon, should be avoided in
bear country.*

## To Prepare

1. Heat the broiler to high. Line a small baking sheet
   or broiling pan with aluminum foil, then place the
   salmon fillet on the baking sheet and sprinkle the
   fish with salt and pepper. Broil the salmon for 6 to
   8 minutes, or until the center is just slightly translucent. Remove the salmon from the oven and
   place it on a paper towel–lined plate to absorb
   any extra fat. Use more paper towels to press
   additional fat from the salmon. Allow the salmon
   to cool enough to be able to flake.

CONTINUED >

2. Preheat the oven to 400°F. Line a large baking sheet with foil and spray it lightly with oil. Put the sweet potato, onion, and red bell pepper on the baking sheet, and sprinkle with the salt and pepper. Toss to combine, and if the vegetables look dry, spray them lightly with oil. Roast the vegetables for 10 minutes, remove them from the oven, sprinkle them with the paprika, toss to mix, and return to the oven to roast for another 7 to 10 minutes until the sweet potatoes are quite tender. Remove the baking sheet from the oven and transfer all the vegetables to a large bowl.

3. Add the flaked salmon to the bowl. Add the dill and parsley and toss to combine.

**To Dehydrate**

1. Spread the hash out evenly on the dehydrator trays fitted with a solid plastic tray insert.

2. Place the trays in the dehydrator. Set the dehydrator to 145°F and turn it on. If your dehydrator has a built-in timer, set it for 7 hours. For models without a timer, set a separate timer.

3. At the 7-hour mark, check the hash. The vegetables should be firm without feeling moist. The salmon should be a bit crumbly. If necessary, continue to dry the hash for another 1 to 2 hours.

### To Store

Measure the total amount of hash, divide it into four portions, and place each potion in a boil-in bag. Label and date the bags. Store for up to 6 months.

### To Rehydrate

Add ½ cup of boiling water to the bag. Mix it well, cover, and let it sit for about 15 minutes. Stir the hash again before eating.

**NUTRITIONAL INFORMATION (PER SERVING):** 390 calories, 8g fat, 40g carb, 38g protein, 810mg sodium (34% DV).

## Ingredient Tip

For a spot of piquant flavor in this rich breakfast dish, consider adding 2 tablespoons of capers to the hash before you put it in the dehydrator.

# MEDITERRANEAN TOFU SCRAMBLE

**DAIRY FREE · GLUTEN FREE · NUT FREE · SUGAR FREE · VEGAN**

**DRAINING TIME:** 45 MINUTES  **PREP TIME:** 30 MINUTES
**COOK TIME:** 25 MINUTES  **DEHYDRATION TIME:** 6 TO 8 HOURS  **REHYDRATION TIME:** 15 MINUTES
**WATER NEEDED FOR REHYDRATION (PER SERVING):** ½ CUP

**SERVES:** 4

1 pound soft or silken tofu

¼ teaspoon turmeric

⅜ teaspoon salt, divided

¼ teaspoon freshly ground black pepper, divided

2 teaspoons olive oil

¼ cup minced red onion

1 medium red bell pepper, thinly sliced

1 (8-ounce) bag baby spinach, roughly chopped

⅓ cup chopped pitted Kalamata olives

1 cup artichokes in water, drained and roughly chopped

½ teaspoon dried oregano

*For this protein-packed breakfast, be sure to get silken or soft tofu, as the firmer varieties do not rehydrate well. White beans make a good substitute if you can't find the softer tofu.*

## To Prepare

1. Drain the tofu by placing it on a cutting board that is propped up slightly with a kitchen towel and positioned to drain into the sink. Place a folded paper towel on top of the tofu and a plate on top of the towel. A plate with a bag of rice for some added weight works well. Drain the tofu for at least 45 minutes.

2. Place the drained tofu in a small bowl and add the turmeric, ⅛ teaspoon of salt, and ⅛ teaspoon of pepper. Stir with a fork to mix well.

3. Heat a large nonstick skillet over medium-high heat. Transfer the tofu to the skillet and cook, stirring occasionally, for 3 to 4 minutes. This will dry the tofu out just a bit more. Remove the tofu from the skillet and set it aside.

4. Return the skillet to medium-high heat and pour in the oil. Add the onion and cook for 1 to 2 minutes until the onion has softened slightly. Add the bell pepper and cook for 2 more minutes. Add the spinach, stir to mix, cover the skillet, and cook for 3 to 4 minutes or until the spinach has wilted. Reduce the heat to medium, and add the olives, artichoke hearts, oregano, and the remaining ¼ teaspoon of salt and remaining ⅛ teaspoon of pepper. Stir to combine. Cook for 3 to 4 minutes then add the tofu. Stir to combine and cook for 3 to 4 minutes more.

**To Dehydrate**
1. Spread the scramble out evenly on the dehydrator trays fitted with a solid plastic tray insert.
2. Place the trays in the dehydrator. Set the dehydrator to 135°F and turn it on. If your dehydrator has a built-in timer, set it for 6 hours. For models without a timer, set a separate timer.
3. At the 6-hour mark, check the scramble. The vegetables should be firm and should not feel moist. If necessary, continue to dry the scramble for another 1 to 2 hours.

CONTINUED ➤

## To Store

Measure the total amount of scramble, divide it into four portions, and place each portion in a boil-in bag. Label and date the bags. Store for up to 12 months.

## To Rehydrate

Add ½ cup of boiling water to the bag. Mix it well, cover, and let it sit for about 15 minutes. Stir the scramble again before eating.

**NUTRITIONAL INFORMATION (PER SERVING):** 370 calories, 13g fat, 45g carb, 17g protein, 1260mg sodium (53% DV).

## Note

If you are using white beans in place of tofu, rinse and drain 1 (15-ounce) can of small white beans, mix them with the turmeric, salt, and pepper, and set it aside. Add the beans to the scramble at the same time you add the olives and artichoke hearts.

# SMOKY RED BEAN AND BACON WRAPS

**DAIRY FREE • GLUTEN FREE • NUT FREE • SOY FREE • SUGAR FREE**

**PREP TIME:** 30 MINUTES  **COOK TIME:** 40 MINUTES  **DEHYDRATION TIME:** 7 TO 9 HOURS
**REHYDRATION TIME:** 15 MINUTES  **WATER NEEDED FOR REHYDRATION (PER SERVING):** ¾ CUP

**SERVES:** 4

## For the rice

1 teaspoon olive oil

¼ cup minced onion

¾ cup basmati rice

1½ cups chicken broth

## For the beans

4 thick bacon slices, cut into 1-inch-wide pieces

1 cup diced onions (½-inch dice)

4 celery stalks, cut into ¼-inch pieces

1 garlic clove, minced

1 medium bell pepper, cut into ½-inch dice

1 (15-ounce) can small red beans, rinsed and drained

¼ teaspoon smoked paprika

¼ teaspoon freshly ground black pepper

⅛ teaspoon cayenne pepper

½ cup water

2 tablespoons minced fresh flat leaf parsley

*Slightly spicy with a hint of smoky flavors, red beans and bacon with rice can be served in a wrap or on its own. Look for Black Forest bacon to enhance the smoky flavor.*

### To Make the Rice

1. Preheat the oven to 350°F. Heat the oil in a large nonstick skillet over medium heat. Add the onion and sauté briefly, 1 to 2 minutes, until the onion is soft. Add the rice and cook, stirring, for 3 to 4 minutes until the rice starts to turn opaque and has some golden color.

2. Transfer the mixture to a 9-inch square glass baking dish and pour the broth over the rice. Stir to mix in the broth, cover the dish with aluminum foil, and bake for 30 minutes. Remove the dish from the oven and set it aside.

CONTINUED >

**To Make the Beans**

1. While the rice is baking, wipe your skillet and place it over medium-high heat. Put the bacon in the skillet and cook it for 7 to 9 minutes, stirring occasionally, until the bacon is crispy and the fat is rendered. Remove the bacon with a slotted spoon and transfer it to a paper towel–lined plate to drain. Use more paper towels to press as much fat out of the bacon as possible.

2. Return the skillet to medium heat, leaving 2 teaspoons of bacon fat in the skillet. Add the onions and celery and cook for 2 to 3 minutes until the vegetables start to soften. Add the garlic and bell pepper and cook for 2 to 3 minutes until the peppers soften.

3. Reduce the heat to medium-low, and add the beans, paprika, pepper, and cayenne to the skillet. Stir to mix and add ½ cup of water. Simmer the beans gently for 15 to 20 minutes until the liquid has reduced and thickened, and the beans are soft when mashed with a spoon. If necessary, add another ¼ cup of water to the mix to keep it simmering. Remove the skillet from the heat and stir in the bacon and parsley.

**To Dehydrate**

1.  Spread the bean mix out evenly on the dehydrator trays fitted with a solid plastic insert, making sure that any liquid in the mix is included on the trays. Spread the rice out on separate trays.

2.  Place the trays in the dehydrator. Set the dehydrator to 135°F and turn it on. If your dehydrator has a built-in timer, set it for 7 hours. For models without a timer, set a separate timer.

3.  At the 7-hour mark, check the vegetables and rice. The vegetables should be firm and should not feel moist. If necessary, continue to dry them for another 1 to 2 hours. Keep in mind that rice will dry more quickly than vegetables, so remove the rice when it is dry and hard to the touch.

**To Store**

Measure the total amount of beans and rice separately. Divide both the beans and rice into four portions and place one portion of each into four boil-in bags. Label and date the bags. Store for up to 6 months.

CONTINUED ➤

**To Rehydrate**

Add ¾ cup of boiling water to the bag. Mix it well, cover, and let sit for about 15 minutes. Stir the rice and beans again and wrap them into a tortilla, if using, before eating.

**NUTRITIONAL INFORMATION (PER SERVING, WITH TORTILLA):**
590 calories, 19g fat, 80g carb, 20g protein, 1130mg sodium (47% DV).

## Ingredient Tip

Small red beans work better than kidney beans, which will split open during the drying process.

# Beverages

Although these three recipes don't require dehydration, they are beverages you can make for the trail using already-dried ingredients.

# POWER SHAKE

**GLUTEN FREE · SOY FREE**

**SERVES:** 8

¾ cup whole milk powder or milk powder of your choice

½ cup instant coffee such as Starbucks VIA (4 packets)

¼ cup chocolate instant breakfast drink mix

*This drink is for those who just want to get moving in the morning. It will get you a few miles down the trail until you are ready to stop for breakfast.*

1. Combine the milk powder, coffee, and chocolate mix in a zip-sealed bag, close the bag, and shake it to mix.
2. To prepare the shake, combine 2½ tablespoons power mix with 8 ounces of cool water, stir, and drink.

# SPICY COCOA

**GLUTEN FREE • SOY FREE**

**SERVES:** 9

1¾ cups whole milk powder

½ cup coconut sugar

¼ cup Dutch processed cocoa

¾ teaspoon ground ginger

¾ teaspoon ground cinnamon

¼ teaspoon cayenne pepper

¼ teaspoon salt

*Warm in more than one way, this drink is both comforting and invigorating.*

1. Combine the milk powder, sugar, cocoa, ginger, cinnamon, cayenne, and salt in a zip-sealed bag, close the bag, and shake it to mix.
2. To prepare the cocoa, combine 3 tablespoons of cocoa mix with 8 ounces of boiling water, stir, and drink.

# COCONUT CHAI

**GLUTEN FREE · SOY FREE**

**SERVES:** 12

1¼ cups coconut milk powder

1½ tablespoons coconut sugar

2 teaspoons ground cinnamon

1¼ teaspoons ground ginger

1 teaspoon ground cardamom

¾ teaspoon ground cloves

½ teaspoon ground nutmeg

*This creamy, coconut-based drink is like a chai steamer for the trail.*

1. Combine the coconut milk powder, sugar, cinnamon, ginger, cardamom, cloves, and nutmeg in a zip-sealed bag, close the bag, and shake it to mix.
2. To prepare the chai, combine 2 tablespoons of chai mix with 8 ounces of boiling water, stir, and drink.

CHAPTER SEVEN

# LUNCH AND DINNER

The recipes in this chapter provide a wide variety of options for your trailside meals. The chapter starts with cold-soak salads. These are an excellent choice for lunch because there's no need to unpack your stove and set up your kitchen midday. Simply add a couple ounces of cool water to a dehydrated salad, and 10 to 15 minutes later you will have a refreshing meal. Conversely, if you want a hot lunch, there are soups and stews to warm you up, and there are options for omnivores and vegetarians alike.

# SESAME GINGER KALE SLAW (COLD SOAK)

**DAIRY FREE** · **GLUTEN FREE** · **VEGAN FRIENDLY**

**PREP TIME:** 30 MINUTES  **DEHYDRATION TIME:** 8 TO 10 HOURS

**REHYDRATION TIME:** 15 MINUTES  **WATER NEEDED TO REHYDRATE (PER SERVING):** ¼ CUP

**SERVES:** 4

4 tablespoons rice vinegar

2 tablespoons vegetable oil

1 tablespoon soy sauce
or tamari

1 teaspoon sesame oil

1 teaspoon crushed
ginger root

1 (packed) teaspoon
brown sugar

1 tablespoon sesame seeds

3 cups shredded
red cabbage

3 cups stemmed and
roughly chopped kale

1 yellow bell pepper, cut into
½-inch dice

4 scallions, thinly sliced

¼ cup chopped
fresh cilantro

1 (10-ounce) can mandarin
oranges, drained and
roughly chopped

1 (10-ounce) can chicken,
drained and flaked
(optional)

**To pack for the trail**

½ cup sliced almonds

*This cold-soak salad has a bright flavor that will be an easy lunch for you on the trail. You can add chicken to the salad if you like, and the almond topping provides a great crunch.*

## To Prepare

1. In a small bowl, combine the vinegar, vegetable oil, soy sauce, sesame oil, ginger, sugar, and sesame seeds and stir to mix thoroughly. Set the dressing aside.

2. In a large bowl, combine the cabbage, kale, bell pepper, scallions, cilantro, mandarin oranges, and chicken (if using) and mix thoroughly. If you choose to include the chicken, make sure it is thoroughly flaked, as bigger chunks will not rehydrate well. Add the dressing to the salad and mix the slaw again.

## To Dehydrate

1. Spread the slaw out evenly on the dehydrator trays fitted with a solid plastic insert, making sure that the dressing is distributed evenly between all the trays.

CONTINUED ➤

2. Place the trays in the dehydrator. Set the dehydrator to 140°F and turn it on. If your dehydrator has a built-in timer, set it for 8 hours. For models without a timer, set a separate timer.

3. At the 8-hour mark, check the vegetables. The bell peppers and mandarins should be firm and should not feel moist. If necessary, continue to dry the slaw for another 1 to 2 hours.

**To Store**

Measure the total amount of slaw, divide it into four portions, and place each portion in a zip-sealed bag. Divide the almonds into 4 small bags and place one bag inside each slaw bag. Label and date the bags. Store for up to one 1 year.

**To Rehydrate (per serving)**

Remove the bag of almonds and add ¼ cup of cool water to the slaw bag. Mix the slaw well, cover, and let it sit for about 15 minutes. Stir the slaw again and top it with the almonds before eating.

**NUTRITIONAL INFORMATION (PER SERVING, WITH CHICKEN):**
380 calories, 22g fat, 25g carb, 24g protein, 590mg sodium (25% DV).

# LEMONY LENTIL SALAD (COLD SOAK)

**DAIRY FREE** • **GLUTEN FREE** • **NUT FREE** • **SOY FREE** • **VEGAN**

**PREP TIME:** 30 MINUTES  **COOK TIME:** 30 MINUTES
**DEHYDRATION TIME:** 6 TO 8 HOURS  **REHYDRATION TIME:** 15 TO 20 MINUTES
**WATER NEEDED FOR REHYDRATION (PER SERVING):** SCANT ½ CUP

**SERVES:** 4

4 tablespoons olive oil

3 tablespoons rice vinegar, unseasoned

4 tablespoons freshly squeezed lemon juice

2 teaspoons lemon zest

1 teaspoon agave, or ½ teaspoon sugar

½ teaspoon dried thyme

¾ teaspoon salt, divided

¼ teaspoon freshly ground black pepper

1½ cups lentils, picked over and rinsed

3 celery stalks, cut into ½-inch dice

1 yellow bell pepper, cut into ½-inch dice

½ cup matchstick carrots

¼ cup chopped fresh flat leaf parsley

*Lentils are a great plant-based source of protein and are quite filling as well. This salad makes the perfect trailside lunch or side dish to share at dinner time.*

## To Prepare

1. In a small bowl, combine the oil, vinegar, lemon juice, lemon zest, agave, thyme, ¼ teaspoon of salt, and the pepper. Mix thoroughly and set the dressing aside.

2. Put the lentils and the remaining ½ teaspoon of salt in a medium pot over medium-high heat. Cover the lentils with the water and bring the water to a boil. Partially cover the pot and reduce the heat to a gentle simmer. If needed, add another cup of water while the lentils are cooking. Cook the lentils for 25 to 30 minutes or until they are soft but not mushy. Drain the lentils, rinse them in cold water, and set them aside to cool.

CONTINUED ⟩

3. When the lentils are cool, transfer them to a large bowl with the celery, bell pepper, carrots, and parsley. Place all the vegetables in a large bowl.
4. Add the dressing to the vegetables and mix well to combine.

**To Dehydrate**

1. Spread the salad out evenly on the dehydrator trays fitted with a solid plastic insert.
2. Place the trays in the dehydrator. Set the dehydrator to 135°F and turn it on. If your dehydrator has a built-in timer, set it for 6 hours. For models without a timer, set a separate timer.
3. At the 6-hour mark, check the vegetables. They should be firm and should not feel moist. If necessary, continue to dry the salad for another 1 to 2 hours.

### To Store

Measure the total amount of salad, divide it into four portions, and place each portion in a zip-sealed bag. Label and date the bags. Store for up to 1 year.

### To Rehydrate

Add a scant ½ cup of cool water to the bag. Mix it well, cover, and let it sit for 15 to 20 minutes. Stir the salad again before eating.

**NUTRITIONAL INFORMATION (PER SERVING)**: 410 calories, 15g fat, 53g carb, 20g protein, 670mg sodium (28% DV).

## Rehydration Tip

This lentil salad produces what may look like a very low yield, but remember how nutritionally dense lentils are; even though the portion looks small, it still packs a nutritional punch.

# BLACK BEAN AND CORN COUSCOUS SALAD (COLD SOAK)

**MEAT FREE · NUT FREE · SOY FREE · SUGAR FREE · VEGAN FRIENDLY**

**PREP TIME:** 25 MINUTES  **COOK TIME:** 5 MINUTES
**DEHYDRATION TIME:** 6 TO 8 HOURS  **REHYDRATION TIME:** 15 TO 20 MINUTES
**WATER NEEDED TO REHYDRATE (PER SERVING):** ½ CUP

**SERVES:** 4

1½ cups water

3 tablespoons oil, divided

½ teaspoon salt

1 cup couscous

Freshly squeezed juice from 3 limes

2 tablespoons rice vinegar

½ teaspoon ground cumin

½ teaspoon chili powder

¼ teaspoon freshly ground black pepper

1 (15-ounce) can black beans, rinsed and drained

1 cup white corn kernels, fresh or frozen (thaw if using frozen)

2 cups diced zucchini

¼ cup minced fresh cilantro

½ cup queso fresco cheese, finely crumbled (optional)

**To pack for trail**

½ cup roasted and salted pepitas (pumpkin seeds)

*This salad makes a delicious trailside lunch. A cold-soak salad doesn't require hot water to rehydrate, so you needn't unpack anything more than the salad and a fork. The zesty dressing complements the beans and zucchini nicely to make a satisfying meal, and the pepitas sprinkled on top provide the perfect crunch.*

## To Prepare

1. In a medium pot, combine the water, 1 tablespoon of oil, and the salt and bring to a boil. Remove the pot from the heat, add the couscous, and stir to mix. Cover the pot and let it sit for 5 minutes. Fluff the couscous with a fork and transfer it to a large bowl.

2. In a small bowl, mix the remaining 2 tablespoons of oil, the lime juice, rice vinegar, cumin, chili powder, and black pepper. Set the dressing aside.

3. Add the black beans, corn, zucchini, and cilantro to the bowl containing the couscous. Stir to mix, then add the dressing and cheese (if using). Stir well.

**To Dehydrate**
1. Spread the salad out evenly on the dehydrator trays fitted with a solid plastic insert.
2. Place the trays in the dehydrator. Set the dehydrator to 135°F and turn it on. If your dehydrator has a built-in timer, set it for 6 hours. For models without a timer, set a separate timer.
3. At the 6-hour mark, check the vegetables. The zucchini and beans should be hard to the touch and should not feel moist. If necessary, continue to dry the salad for another 1 to 2 hours.

**To Store**
Measure the total amount of salad, divide it into four portions, and place each portion in a boil-in bag. Divide the pepitas into 4 small zip-sealed bags and place one inside each salad bag. Label and date the bags. Store for up to 1 year.

CONTINUED >

### To Rehydrate

Remove the small bag of pepitas. Add ½ cup of cool water to the salad bag. Mix it well, cover, and let it sit for 15 to 20 minutes. Stir the salad again, and sprinkle the pepitas over the top, before eating.

**NUTRITIONAL INFORMATION (PER SERVING)**: 530 calories, 23 fat, 65g carb, 22g protein, 680mg sodium (28% DV).

## Dehydration Tip

If you are using the cheese, make certain to crumble it finely; it will not rehydrate well if left in big chunks.

# SPLIT PEA SOUP WITH BACON AND ROSEMARY

**DAIRY FREE** • **GLUTEN FREE** • **NUT FREE** • **SOY FREE** • **SUGAR FREE**

**PREP TIME:** 20 MINUTES  **COOK TIME:** 35 MINUTES

**DEHYDRATION TIME:** 6 TO 8 HOURS  **REHYDRATION TIME:** 15 MINUTES

**WATER NEEDED FOR REHYDRATION (PER SERVING):** 1½ CUPS

**SERVES:** 4

4 thick bacon slices, cut into 1-inch pieces

1 onion, cut into ¼-inch dice

1 garlic clove, minced

1½ cups split peas, rinsed and drained

5 cups chicken broth or water

1 tablespoon fresh rosemary leaves or 1 teaspoon dried rosemary

3 carrots, cut into ¼-inch rounds

*A hearty soup, such as this split pea soup, is comforting at the end of a long day on the trail. The rosemary adds a hit of peppery lemon flavor and complexity to an otherwise simple soup.*

## To Prepare

1. Heat a medium pot over medium heat. Place the bacon in the pot and cook until the fat has rendered and the bacon is crisp, 5 to 6 minutes. Transfer the bacon to a paper towel–lined plate to drain, and use more paper towels to press out as much fat from the bacon as possible.

2. Discard all but 2 teaspoons of bacon fat, and return the pot with the reserved bacon fat to medium heat.

3. Add the onion and garlic to the pot and continue cooking for 2 to 3 minutes or until the onion starts to soften.

CONTINUED ➢

4. Add the split peas, broth, and rosemary. Raise the heat to medium high to bring the broth to a simmer, then lower the heat to medium-low, cover the pot, and cook the soup for 15 minutes.

5. Return the bacon to the pot and add the carrots. Cook, covered, for another 10 minutes.

6. The soup is done when the split peas are soft and the carrots are just fork tender.

**To Dehydrate**

1. Pour the soup onto dehydrator trays fitted with a solid plastic tray insert.

2. Place the trays in the dehydrator. Set the dehydrator to 140°F and turn it on. If your dehydrator has a built-in timer, set it for 6 hours. For models without a timer, set a separate timer.

3. At the 6-hour mark, check the soup. The carrots and bacon should be firm and should not feel moist. If necessary, continue to dry the soup for another 1 to 2 hours.

### To Store

Measure the total amount of soup, divide it into four portions, and place each portion in a boil-in bag. Label and date the bags. Store for up to 6 months.

### To Rehydrate

Add 1½ cups of boiling water to the bag. Mix it well, cover, and let it sit for about 15 minutes. Stir the soup again before eating.

**NUTRITIONAL INFORMATION (PER SERVING)**: 570 calories, 23g fat, 56g carb, 36g protein, 1180mg sodium (49% DV).

# SPICY SWEET POTATO AND CHORIZO STEW

**DAIRY FREE** · **NUT FREE** · **SOY FREE** · **SUGAR FREE**

**PREP TIME:** 35 MINUTES  **COOK TIME:** 50 MINUTES

**DEHYDRATION TIME:** 7 TO 9 HOURS  **REHYDRATION TIME:** 20 TO 25 MINUTES

**WATER NEEDED FOR REHYDRATION (PER SERVING):** 1 CUP

**SERVES:** 4

3 cups diced sweet potatoes (¾-inch dice)

1 tablespoon olive oil

Salt

Freshly ground black pepper

8 ounces chorizo sausage

1 cup diced onion (½-inch dice)

½ teaspoon minced garlic

4 cups chicken broth or water

1 (15-ounce) can black beans, rinsed and drained

⅛ teaspoon ground cinnamon

¼ cup roughly chopped fresh cilantro

Juice of half a lime

*The fragrant chorizo combined with earthy black beans and sweet potatoes are enlivened with a burst of tartness from the lime juice. This stew is warming in more than one way.*

## To Prepare

1. Preheat the oven to 425°F. Line a baking sheet with aluminum foil and spread the sweet potatoes on the baking sheet. Toss the potatoes with the oil and season with salt and pepper. Roast for 11 to 13 minutes, turning the potatoes halfway through for even browning.

2. When the potatoes have started to turn brown and are just fork tender, remove them from the oven and set them aside.

3. Heat a Dutch oven or soup pot over medium-high heat. Put the chorizo in the pot and cook it for 10 minutes, breaking the sausage into small crumbles. Use a slotted spoon to transfer the sausage to a paper towel–lined plate to drain. Use more paper towels to press as much fat as possible out of the sausage.

4. Return the pot to medium heat. If necessary, add more oil to make 2 teaspoons of fat in the pot. Add the onion and cook for 2 to 3 minutes until it starts to turn translucent. Add the garlic and cook, stirring constantly, for 30 seconds.

5. Add the broth to the pot, scraping the bottom of the pot with a wooden spoon to deglaze it, bringing up any browned bits from the sausage. Add the sweet potatoes, black beans, sausage, and cinnamon to the pot. Bring the stew to a simmer then lower the heat to a gentle simmer and cook, uncovered, for 20 minutes.

6. Remove the stew from the heat, add the cilantro and lime juice, and stir to combine.

**To Dehydrate**

1. Spread the stew out on the dehydrator trays fitted with a solid plastic tray insert.

2. Place the trays in the dehydrator. Set the dehydrator to 145°F and turn it on. If your dehydrator has a built-in timer, set it for 7 hours. For models without a timer, set a separate timer.

3. At the 7-hour mark, check the stew. The sweet potatoes and beans should be firm and should not feel moist. If necessary, continue to dry the stew for another 1 to 2 hours.

CONTINUED >

**To Store**

Measure the total amount of stew, divide it into four portions, and place each portion in a boil-in bag. Label and date the bags. Store for up to 6 months.

**To Rehydrate**

Add 1 cup of boiling water to the bag. Mix the stew well, cover, and let it sit for 20 to 25 minutes. Stir the stew again before eating.

**NUTRITIONAL INFORMATION (PER SERVING)**: 500 calories, 26g fat, 45g carb, 23g protein, 1340mg sodium (56% DV).

## Ingredient Tip

If you don't have access to chorizo, choose another spicy pork sausage to substitute. Avoid packaged tubes of chorizo; the consistency of this variety is too thin for this recipe. Make sure the sausage is crumbled into small pieces for proper rehydration.

# PORTER-INFUSED CHILI WITH BACON

**DAIRY FREE** • **NUT FREE** • **SOY FREE** • **SUGAR FREE**
**PREP TIME:** 20 MINUTES  **COOK TIME:** 1 HOUR
**DEHYDRATION TIME:** 6 TO 8 HOURS  **REHYDRATION TIME:** 15 TO 20 MINUTES
**WATER NEEDED TO REHYDRATE (PER SERVING):** ¾ CUP
**SERVES:** 4

1 pound ground beef, at least 90 percent lean

3 thick bacon slices, cut into 1-inch pieces

1 medium onion, cut into ½-inch dice

2 garlic cloves, minced

12 ounces beer, preferably porter or stout

1 (15-ounce) can black beans, rinsed and drained

1 (15-ounce) can petite diced tomatoes, with juice

1½ teaspoons chili powder

1 teaspoon ground cumin

¼ teaspoon freshly ground black pepper

¼ teaspoon salt

¼ teaspoon red pepper flakes

*This chili is a simple dish, elevated to a new level by the porter. Although you can omit the porter and use 12 ounces of broth or water instead, the porter infuses the chili with a lovely chocolate flavor. This is a great dish for cool evenings on the trail—so warming!*

## To Prepare

1. Heat a medium pot over medium heat and put the ground beef in the pot. With a wooden spoon, break the beef into small crumbles. The beef pieces need to be small in order to rehydrate well. Cook the beef for 6 to 7 minutes or until it is cooked through. Use a slotted spoon to transfer the beef to a paper towel–lined plate to drain.

2. Discard any accumulated liquids from the pot and return the pot to the heat. Add the bacon and cook, stirring occasionally, for 5 to 6 minutes or until the fat is rendered and the bacon is starting to

CONTINUED ➤

crisp. Use a slotted spoon to transfer the bacon to a paper towel–lined plate to drain. Reserve 1 tablespoon of the bacon fat and discard any extra.

3. Return the pot to the heat and add the onion to the reserved bacon fat. Cook, stirring occasionally, for 2 minutes or until the onion just starts to soften. Add the garlic and cook for 30 seconds, stirring constantly.

4. Return the beef to the pot. Add the beer and allow the foam to subside, then stir and bring to a gentle simmer for 6 to 8 minutes.

5. Add the beans, tomatoes, chili powder, cumin, pepper, salt, and red pepper flakes to the pot. Stir to mix and bring to a simmer. Once simmering, lower the heat to medium-low and simmer for 20 minutes.

6. After 20 minutes, return the bacon to the pot, taste the chili, and adjust the seasonings. Simmer for another 10 minutes.

**To Dehydrate**

1. Spread the chili out on dehydrator trays fitted with a solid plastic insert, making sure that all the liquid in the chili has been evenly distributed across the trays.

2. Place the trays in the dehydrator. Set the dehydrator to 145°F and turn it on. If your dehydrator has a built-in timer, set it for 6 hours. For models without a timer, set a separate timer.

3. At the 6-hour mark, check the chili. Both the beans and the beef should be hard to the touch and the vegetables should be firm. If necessary, continue to dry the chili for another 1 to 2 hours.

**To Store**

Measure the total amount of chili, divide it into four portions, and place each portion in a boil-in bag. Label and date the bags. Store for up to 6 months.

**To Rehydrate**

Add ¾ cup of boiling water to the bag. Mix it well, cover, and let it sit for 15 to 20 minutes. Stir the chili again before eating.

**NUTRITIONAL INFORMATION (PER SERVING)**: 430 calories, 16g fat, 29g carb, 35g protein, 1080mg sodium (45% DV).

## Tip

Consider making a batch of cornbread to go with the chili. Bake the cornbread and when cool, crumble 1 cup of cornbread onto a dehydrator tray. Once dry (3 to 5 hours), divide the crumbles into four portions and place each portion in a zip-sealed bag. Put one crumbles bag in each chili bag. When you are ready to rehydrate the chili, remove the bag of crumbles first, and then when the chili is rehydrated, sprinkle the crumbles over the top. Yum.

# WHITE BEAN CHICKEN STEW WITH GRILLED POBLANOS

**GLUTEN FREE • NUT FREE • SOY FREE • SUGAR FREE**

**PREP TIME:** 25 MINUTES   **COOK TIME:** 45 MINUTES

**DEHYDRATION TIME:** 7 TO 9 HOURS   **REHYDRATION TIME:** 20 TO 25 MINUTES

**WATER NEEDED FOR REHYDRATION (PER SERVING):** 1¼ CUPS

**SERVES:** 6

2 medium poblano peppers

1 pound skinless boneless chicken thighs, trimmed of fat

¼ teaspoon salt

¼ teaspoon freshly ground black pepper

1½ tablespoons chili powder

2 tablespoons olive oil

½ cup diced onions (½-inch dice)

2 garlic cloves, minced

4 cups chicken broth

2 (15-ounce) cans small white beans, rinsed and drained

½ cup chopped fresh cilantro

1½ cups shredded Monterey Jack cheese

Juice of 1 lime

*Freshly grilled peppers are a great addition to this soup, and the poblanos can be substituted with Anaheim or Pasilla peppers. To save some prep time, feel free to substitute a small can of chopped green chiles.*

## To Prepare

1. Heat the broiler to high. Place the peppers on a baking sheet covered in aluminum foil and set the sheet on the oven shelf 4 inches under the broiler. Broil the peppers for 6 to 7 minutes, turning them occasionally to char the skin on all sides. Remove the peppers from the oven and wrap them in the foil to steam the skin. Set them aside to cool.

2. While the peppers cool, cut the larger chicken thighs into two pieces, pat them dry, and sprinkle them with the salt, pepper, and chili powder.

3. Heat a Dutch oven or soup pot over medium-high heat. Pour the oil into the pot and add the chicken thighs when the oil is shimmering but not smoking. Cook the thighs without moving them for 5 to

6 minutes, then turn the thighs over and cook them for another 5 to 6 minutes until they are cooked through. Transfer the thighs to a paper towel–lined plate to drain and set them aside to cool slightly.

4. Remove all but 2 teaspoons of oil from the pot and return the pot to medium heat. Add the onion and cook, stirring occasionally for 3 to 4 minutes, until it starts to soften. Add the garlic and cook for a further 30 seconds.

5. Add the broth to the pot and scrape the bottom of the pot with a wooden spoon to loosen any browned bits of chicken. Add the beans and bring the broth to a gentle simmer.

6. Holding the peppers under cold running water, pull the skins off carefully. Pull the stem and core out of each pepper and slit them open to rinse off the seeds. Cut the peppers into ½-inch dice and add them to the pot.

7. Shred the chicken thighs and return them to the pot. Bring the soup back to a simmer and cook for 20 minutes.

8. Remove the pot from the heat and add the cilantro, cheese, and lime juice.

**To Dehydrate**

1. Spread the stew out on the dehydrator trays fitted with a solid plastic tray insert.

CONTINUED ➤

2. Place the trays in the dehydrator. Set the dehydrator to 145°F and turn it on. If your dehydrator has a built-in timer, set it for 7 hours. For models without a timer, set a separate timer.

3. At the 7-hour mark, check the stew. The vegetables should be firm and should not feel moist. If necessary, continue to dry the stew for another 1 to 2 hours.

**To Store**

Measure the total amount of stew, divide it into six portions, and place each portion in a boil-in bag. Label and date the bags. Store for up to 6 months.

**To Rehydrate**

Add 1¼ cups of boiling water to a bag. Mix it well, cover, and let it sit for 20 to 25 minutes. Stir the stew again before eating.

**NUTRITIONAL INFORMATION (PER SERVING)**: 430 calories, 14g fat, 42g carb, 35g protein, 520mg sodium (22% DV).

**Ingredient Tip**

Shred the chicken into much smaller pieces than you might normally. Chicken doesn't rehydrate as easily as other meats, so smaller pieces will help speed up the rehydration process. This stew may need a bit more time to rehydrate than other soups.

# TUNA SALAD WRAPS (COLD SOAK)

**DAIRY FREE · GLUTEN FREE · NUT FREE · SOY FREE · SUGAR FREE**

**PREP TIME:** 20 MINUTES **DEHYDRATION TIME:** 6 TO 8 HOURS **REHYDRATION TIME:** 15 MINUTES
**WATER NEEDED FOR REHYDRATION (PER SERVING):** ⅓ CUP

**SERVES:** 4

2 (7-ounce) cans solid water-packed tuna, drained

2 tablespoons olive oil

2 tablespoons capers, plus 1 tablespoon caper liquid

1 tablespoon Dijon mustard

Freshly ground black pepper

3 cups shredded cabbage

¼ cup chopped fresh flat leaf parsley

¼ cup minced red onion

1 tablespoon chopped fresh dill, or 1 teaspoon dried dill

**To pack for the trail**

4 (8-inch) gluten-free tortillas or wraps (or regular tortillas/wraps if you tolerate gluten)

*This tuna salad will provide great energy for the trail, but if you are headed into bear country, you may want to pack a different meal. Strong-smelling foods such as tuna are a draw for wild animals.*

## To Prepare

1. In a medium bowl, flake the tuna with a fork to break up any large chunks.
2. Add the oil, capers with liquid, and Dijon to the bowl and mix. Taste and adjust the seasonings.
3. Add the cabbage, parsley, onion, and dill to the bowl. Mix to combine well.

## To Dehydrate

1. Spread the tuna out evenly on the dehydrator trays fitted with a solid plastic tray insert.
2. Place the trays in the dehydrator. Set the dehydrator to 145°F and turn it on. If your dehydrator has a built-in timer, set it for 6 hours. For models without a timer, set a separate timer.

CONTINUED ➤

3. At the 6-hour mark, check the tuna (it should be crumbly) and the vegetables (they should be firm and should not feel moist). If necessary, continue to dry the tuna for another 1 to 2 hours.

**To Store**

Measure the total amount of tuna salad, divide it into four portions, and place each portion in a zip-sealed bag. Label and date the bags. Store for up to 6 months.

**To Rehydrate**

Add ⅓ cup of cool water to the bag. Mix it well, cover, and let it sit for about 15 minutes. Stir the salad again, place it in the middle of a tortilla, and roll up the tortilla before eating.

**NUTRITIONAL INFORMATION (PER SERVING, WITH TORTILLA):**
350 calories, 13g fat, 27g carb, 28g protein, 840mg sodium (35% DV).

# ROASTED VEGETABLE AND HUMMUS WRAPS

**DAIRY FREE** · **GLUTEN FREE** · **NUT FREE** · **SOY FREE** · **SUGAR FREE**

**PREP TIME:** 45 MINUTES   **COOK TIME:** 20 MINUTES
**DEHYDRATION TIME:** 7 TO 9 HOURS   **REHYDRATION TIME:** 15 TO 20 MINUTES
**WATER NEEDED FOR REHYDRATION (PER SERVING):** ¼ + ⅓ CUPS

**SERVES:** 6

Olive oil cooking spray

1 small eggplant

2 medium zucchini, halved and cut lengthwise into ¼-inch slices

2 medium red bell peppers, cut lengthwise into 1-inch-wide strips

1 large red onion, cut lengthwise into ½-inch-wide strips

Salt

Freshly ground black pepper

1 recipe Hummus (page 147), flavor of your choice

**To pack for the trail**
6 (8-inch) gluten-free tortillas or wraps (or regular tortillas/wraps if you tolerate gluten)

*This recipe has some flexibility. You can use any vegetables that roast well, such as sweet potatoes or root vegetables, though these may take a bit longer to cook.*

**To Prepare**

1. Preheat the oven to 425°F. Line two baking sheets with aluminum foil and spray the foil lightly with oil.

2. Cut the eggplant in half crosswise, then cut each half lengthwise into ¼-inch slices.

3. Arrange the eggplant, zucchini, bell peppers, and onion in a single layer on the baking sheets, spray them lightly with oil, and sprinkle them with salt and pepper. Roast the vegetables for 15 to 20 minutes, turning them over halfway through the cooking process, until they have started to brown and are fork tender. Remove the vegetables from the oven and set them aside to cool slightly.

CONTINUED ➤

**To Dehydrate**

1. Place the vegetables on the dehydrator trays in a single layer, leaving a little space between the pieces. Spread the hummus in an even layer on the tray inserts. Place a solid tray insert on top of each tray you use for the hummus.

2. Place the trays in the dehydrator. Set the dehydrator to 135°F and turn it on. If your dehydrator has a built-in timer, set it for 7 hours. For models without a timer, set a separate timer.

3. At the 7-hour mark, check the vegetables. They should be firm to the touch and should not feel moist. The hummus will be crackled and dusty. If necessary, continue to dry the vegetables for another 1 to 2 hours. The hummus will dry more quickly than the vegetables; remove the hummus when it is dried.

**To Store**

Place the vegetables and hummus in separate bowls. Measure the total amount of each, and divide each into four portions. Place the vegetables in boil-in bags. Place the hummus in smaller zip-sealed bags and place one hummus bag inside each vegetable bag. Label and date the bags. Store for up to 1 year.

### To Rehydrate

Remove the hummus bag from the vegetable bag, add ⅓ cup of cool water to the hummus bag, and knead it to mix. Add ¼ cup of hot water to the vegetable bag. Mix it well, cover, and let it sit for 15 to 20 minutes. Spread the hummus on a tortilla. There may be a little water left over when vegetables are rehydrated; if so, drain the water before placing the veggies on the tortilla. Then place the vegetables on top of the hummus and roll up the tortilla before eating.

**NUTRITIONAL INFORMATION (PER SERVING)**: 490 calories, 12g fat, 81g carb, 20g protein, 700mg sodium (29% DV).

## Preparation Tip

Do not remove the skin from the zucchini. The skin holds the slices together once rehydrated, so make sure to leave some skin on each piece.

# PASTA WITH SAUSAGE AND BRAISED PEPPERS

**DAIRY FREE · GLUTEN FREE FRIENDLY · NUT FREE · SOY FREE · SUGAR FREE**

**PREP TIME:** 15 MINUTES  **COOK TIME:** 30 MINUTES

**DEHYDRATION TIME:** 8 TO 10 HOURS  **REHYDRATION TIME:** 15 TO 20 MINUTES

**WATER NEEDED FOR REHYDRATION (PER SERVING):** A GENEROUS ½ CUP

**SERVES:** 4

6 ounces penne pasta

¾ pound sweet Italian pork sausage

1 teaspoon olive oil

2 cups sliced onion

2 cups sliced red bell peppers

¼ teaspoon salt

¼ teaspoon freshly ground black pepper

½ teaspoon dried oregano

1 (15-ounce) can diced tomatoes, with juices

*To be honest, this dish doesn't look like much when it comes off the stove, but it's one that my son still talks about years after he first had it on the trail. The flavors meld and become more intense while in the dehydrator, creating a memorable trailside dinner.*

## To Prepare

1. Cook the pasta according to the package directions. Reserve ¼ cup of the pasta water, and then drain the pasta but do not rinse it. Set the pasta aside.

2. Heat a large skillet over medium-high heat. Put the sausage in the skillet and cook it for 7 to 9 minutes until the sausage is cooked through, breaking it into small crumbles as it cooks. Use a slotted spoon to transfer the sausage to a paper towel–lined plate to drain and use more paper towels to press as much fat out of the sausage as possible. Do not wipe out the skillet.

3. Return the skillet to medium-high heat and pour in the oil. Add the onions and peppers and cook, stirring occasionally, for 1 to 2 minutes. Add the salt, pepper, and oregano and cook, stirring occasionally, for 5 to 7 minutes or until the vegetables are soft and starting to get some color.

4. Lower the heat to medium-low and add the tomatoes to the skillet. Cook for 1 minute, then return the sausage to the skillet. Cook, stirring occasionally, for 5 minutes.

5. Add the pasta and reserved water to the skillet, stir, cook for another 3 minutes, and remove from the heat.

**To Dehydrate**

1. Spread the pasta mixture out evenly on dehydrator trays fitted with a solid plastic tray insert.

2. Place the trays in the dehydrator. Set the dehydrator to 140°F and turn it on. If your dehydrator has a built-in timer, set it for 8 hours. For models without a timer, set a separate timer.

3. At the 8-hour mark, check the pasta. The pasta and vegetables should be firm and should not feel moist. If necessary, continue to dry the vegetables for another 1 to 2 hours.

CONTINUED ➤

### To Store

Measure the total amount of pasta, divide it into four portions, and place each portion in a boil-in bag. Label and date the bags. Store for up to 3 months.

### To Rehydrate

Add a little more than ½ cup of boiling water to the bag. Mix it well, cover, and let it sit for 15 to 20 minutes. Stir the pasta again before eating.

**NUTRITIONAL INFORMATION (PER SERVING)**: 520 calories, 29g fat, 45g carb, 19g protein, 1010mg sodium (42% DV).

### Ingredient Tip

Make this dish with brown rice pasta for a gluten-free meal.

# WHITE BEAN AND KALE PASTA

**DAIRY FREE • GLUTEN FREE FRIENDLY • NUT FREE • SOY FREE • SUGAR FREE • VEGAN**

**PREP TIME:** 20 MINUTES **COOK TIME:** 25 MINUTES
**DEHYDRATION TIME:** 7 TO 9 HOURS **REHYDRATION TIME:** 15 TO 20 MINUTES
**WATER NEEDED FOR REHYDRATION (PER SERVING):** 1 CUP

**SERVES:** 4

8 ounces penne pasta (or gluten-free brown rice pasta)

1 tablespoon olive oil

1 garlic clove, minced

4 cups stemmed and chopped kale

2 tablespoons water

¼ teaspoon salt

¼ teaspoon freshly ground black pepper

1 teaspoon dried sage

1 (15-ounce) can petite diced tomatoes, with juice

1 (15-ounce) can white beans, rinsed and drained

*This filling dish will keep you going for miles. Because the high-water content of tomatoes slows the drying time, the small cut of petite diced tomatoes is called for in this recipe.*

**To Prepare**

1. Cook the pasta until al dente according to the package directions. Reserve ¼ cup of the pasta water, and then drain the pasta but do not rinse it. Set the pasta aside.

2. Heat the oil in a large skillet or sauté pan over medium-high heat. Add the garlic and cook, stirring, for 30 seconds until fragrant. Add the kale and 2 tablespoons of water. Cover the skillet with a lid and let the kale wilt for 5 to 6 minutes.

3. Remove the lid and lower the heat to medium. Add the salt, pepper, and sage and stir to mix. Add the tomatoes and beans, cover the skillet, and let it simmer for 6 to 7 minutes.

4. Add the pasta and reserved pasta water to the skillet, stir it well to combine, and remove the skillet from the heat.

CONTINUED ➤

## To Dehydrate

1. Spread the pasta out evenly on dehydrator trays fitted with a solid plastic tray insert.
2. Place the trays in the dehydrator. Set the dehydrator to 140°F and turn it on. If your dehydrator has a built-in timer, set it for 7 hours. For models without a timer, set a separate timer.
3. At the 7-hour mark, check the pasta. The pasta and tomatoes should be firm and should not feel moist. If necessary, continue to dry the vegetables for another 1 to 2 hours.

## To Store

Measure the total amount of pasta, divide it into four portions, and place each portion in a boil-in bag. Label and date the bags. Store for up to 12 months.

## To Rehydrate

Add 1 cup of boiling water to the bag. Mix it well, cover, and let it sit for 15 to 20 minutes. Stir the pasta again before eating.

**NUTRITIONAL INFORMATION (PER SERVING):** 450 calories, 5g fat, 80g carb, 21g protein, 420mg sodium (18% DV).

## Trail Tip

Sprinkle grated Parmesan cheese or nutritional yeast over the pasta once it's rehydrated.

# CILANTRO PESTO PASTA WITH VEGGIES

**DAIRY FREE • GLUTEN FREE FRIENDLY • SOY FREE • SUGAR FREE • VEGAN**

**PREP TIME:** 45 MINUTES  **SOAKING TIME:** 1 TO 12 HOURS  **COOK TIME:** 15 MINUTES
**DEHYDRATION TIME:** 8 TO 10 HOURS  **REHYDRATION TIME:** 20 MINUTES
**WATER NEEDED FOR REHYDRATION (PER SERVING):** 1 CUP

**SERVES:** 4

1 cup raw cashews

½ cup water

2 bunches fresh cilantro, large stems removed

½ cup pine nuts

3 tablespoons olive oil, divided

1 tablespoon freshly squeezed lemon juice

½ teaspoon salt

2 cups broccoli florets, cut into 1-inch pieces

1 cup diced zucchini (½-inch dice)

1 cup frozen peas, thawed

1 cup diced red bell pepper (¼-inch dice)

8 ounces rotini or penne pasta (or gluten-free brown rice pasta)

*Cashew cream makes this vibrant creamy pasta dish vegan. The red bell pepper gives a great pop of red in a sea of green flavors, but you can easily swap out any of the vegetables for one of your favorites.*

1. Soak the cashews in 1 cup of water, uncovered, for up to 12 hours. The longer the cashews soak, the creamier the sauce will be.

2. Drain and rinse the cashews, then place them in a blender with ½ cup of fresh water. Do not reuse the soaking water. Blend the cashews until the sauce is smooth, adding a couple tablespoons of water if needed. Set the cream aside.

3. In a blender, purée the cilantro, pine nuts, 2½ tablespoons of oil, the lemon juice, and salt until smooth. Add the pesto to the cashew cream, stir to mix, and set it aside.

CONTINUED ➤

4. Pour an inch of water into a large skillet or sauté pan and heat over medium-high heat until the water is simmering. Add the broccoli and cook for 1 minute. Drain the water and add the remaining 1½ teaspoons of oil and the zucchini to the skillet, stir to coat the zucchini, and cook over medium-high heat for 2 minutes. Transfer the zucchini to a large bowl. Add the peas and bell pepper to the bowl.

5. Cook the pasta according to the package directions. Reserve ¼ cup of the pasta water, and then drain the pasta but do not rinse it. Add the pasta and reserved water to the bowl with the vegetables.

6. Add the pesto cream to the pasta and vegetables and stir to combine.

**To Dehydrate**

1. Spread the pasta out on the dehydrator trays fitted with a solid plastic tray insert, making sure that the sauce is evenly distributed among the trays.

2. Place the trays in the dehydrator. Set the dehydrator to 140°F and turn it on. If your dehydrator has a built-in timer, set it for 8 hours. For models without a timer, set a separate timer.

3. At the 8-hour mark, check the pasta. The broccoli and bell peppers should be firm and should not feel moist. If necessary, continue to dry the pasta for another 1 to 2 hours.

### To Store

Measure the total amount of pasta, divide it into four portions, and place each portion in a boil-in bag. Label and date the bags. Store for up to 1 year.

### To Rehydrate

Add 1 cup of boiling water to the boil-in bag. Mix it well, cover, and let it sit for about 20 minutes. Stir the pasta again before eating.

**NUTRITIONAL INFORMATION (PER SERVING)**: 650 calories, 37g fat, 63g carb, 19g protein, 610mg sodium (25% DV).

## Preparation Tip

A blender will yield creamier results for the cashew cream than a food processor will, but a food processor can certainly be used.

# SALMON AND MUSHROOM COUSCOUS PILAF

**NUT FREE • SOY FREE • SUGAR FREE**

**PREP TIME:** 25 MINUTES **COOK TIME:** 30 MINUTES **DEHYDRATION TIME:** 8 TO 10 HOURS
**REHYDRATION TIME:** 15 MINUTES **WATER NEEDED FOR REHYDRATION (PER SERVING):** 1 CUP
**SERVES:** 4

2 cups chicken broth

4 teaspoons olive oil, divided

1½ cups couscous

3 tablespoons freshly squeezed lemon juice

2 teaspoons lemon zest

⅓ cup plain 5 percent fat Greek yogurt

1 (12-ounce) skinless salmon fillet

¼ teaspoon salt, plus more for seasoning salmon

⅛ teaspoon freshly ground black pepper, plus more for seasoning salmon

2 tablespoons minced shallots

2½ cups sliced white or cremini mushrooms

1 cup quartered grape tomatoes

1 (10-ounce) bag spinach, roughly chopped

*The mushrooms and spinach give this pilaf earthy notes, the tomatoes provide a burst of sweet, and the yogurt lends a hint of tang. Remember that if you're heading into bear territory, foods with strong odors, such as the salmon in this dish, should be avoided.*

## To Prepare

1. Heat the broth and 2 teaspoons of oil in a medium pot over medium-high heat. Bring the broth to a boil, add the couscous, stir, remove the pot from the heat, and cover the pot. Let the couscous sit for 5 minutes, then add the lemon juice, lemon zest, and yogurt. Stir with a fork to mix and set aside.

2. Heat the broiler to high. Line a small baking sheet with aluminum foil and place the salmon on the foil. Sprinkle the fillet with salt and pepper and broil for 5 to 7 minutes until the salmon is still slightly translucent in the center. Do not over-cook. Remove the salmon from the oven and set it aside to cool.

3. Heat the remaining 2 teaspoons of oil in skillet or sauté pan over medium-high heat. Add the shallots and cook, stirring, for 30 seconds. Add the mushrooms and cook, stirring occasionally, for 4 to 6 minutes until they start to release their liquid. Add the tomatoes and cook for 1 minute. Transfer the vegetables and their liquid to a large bowl.

4. Return the skillet to medium heat and put the spinach plus 2 tablespoons of water in the skillet. Cover the skillet and cook for 3 to 4 minutes until the spinach has wilted. Add the spinach to the bowl with the mushrooms and tomatoes.

5. Flake the salmon finely, removing any pin bones you find. Add the salmon and any accumulated juices to the bowl.

6. Add the couscous, salt, and pepper to the bowl and mix until all the ingredients are combined.

**To Dehydrate**

1. Spread the pilaf out evenly on the dehydrator trays fitted with a solid plastic insert.

2. Place the trays in the dehydrator. Set the dehydrator to 145°F and turn it on. If your dehydrator has a built-in timer, set it for 8 hours. For models without a timer, set a separate timer.

CONTINUED ➤

3. At the 8-hour mark, check the pilaf. The tomatoes and salmon should be firm and should not feel moist. If necessary, continue to dry the pilaf for another 1 to 2 hours.

**To Store**

Measure the total amount of pilaf, divide it into four portions, and place each portion in a boil-in bag. Label and date the bags. Store for up to 3 months.

**To Rehydrate**

Add 1 cup of boiling water to the bag. Mix it well, cover, and let it sit for about 15 minutes. Stir the pilaf again before eating.

**NUTRITIONAL INFORMATION (PER SERVING)**: 450 calories, 10g fat, 58g carb, 32g protein, 590mg sodium (25% DV).

# RICE AND BEANS WITH ZUCCHINI AND BELL PEPPER

**DAIRY FREE · GLUTEN FREE · NUT FREE · SOY FREE · SUGAR FREE · VEGAN**

**PREP TIME:** 30 MINUTES  **COOK TIME:** 40 MINUTES
**DEHYDRATION TIME:** 7 TO 9 HOURS  **REHYDRATION TIME:** 15 MINUTES
**WATER NEEDED FOR REHYDRATION (PER SERVING):** 1 CUP
**SERVES:** 4

### For the rice

½ tablespoon oil

½ medium onion, finely chopped

1¼ cups uncooked basmati or long-grain rice

2 cups vegetable stock or water

Salt

Freshly ground black pepper

*This dish is the backbone of my trail meals. It can be dressed up in a variety of ways but is equally fantastic on its own. Try it in a tortilla with some slices of avocado either for breakfast or lunch.*

### To Make the Rice

1. Preheat the oven to 350°F. Heat the oil in a large sauté pan or skillet over medium heat. Add the onion and sauté, stirring occasionally until the onion is slightly tender, about 2 minutes. Add the rice and season with salt and pepper. Stir the mixture frequently, allowing the rice to turn opaque and lightly golden, about 5 minutes. Do not let the rice brown.

2. Put the rice mix into a 9-inch square baking dish, pour the stock or water over it, and cover the dish tightly with aluminum foil. Bake the rice for 30 minutes.

CONTINUED ➤

### For the beans

½ tablespoon oil

½ medium onion, finely chopped

1 garlic clove, minced

1 medium red bell pepper, cut into ¼-inch dice

1 small zucchini, cut into ¼-inch dice

2 (15-ounce) cans black beans, rinsed and drained

¾ cup water

1 teaspoon ground cumin

¼ teaspoon red pepper flakes

2 Roma tomatoes, diced

¼ cup chopped fresh cilantro

### To Make the Beans

1. While the rice is cooking, wipe the pan clean and return it to medium-high heat. Pour in the oil, allow the pan to heat up, and add the onion. Cook, stirring frequently, for 1 minute until the onion starts to turn translucent.

2. Add the garlic and cook for 15 seconds. Add the bell pepper and zucchini and continue cooking, stirring occasionally, for about 3 to 4 minutes until the bell pepper begins to soften.

3. Add the black beans and ¾ cup of water to the pan. Stir to mix, lower the heat to medium, and add the cumin and red pepper flakes. Let the bean mixture simmer for four minutes until the liquid has thickened slightly.

4. Remove the beans from the heat and add the tomatoes and cilantro, stirring briefly to mix. Taste and adjust the seasoning.

### To Dehydrate

1. Spread the beans out on dehydrator trays fitted with a solid plastic insert, making sure that any liquid in the bean mix is included on the trays. Place the rice on separate trays.

2. Place the trays in the dehydrator. Set the dehydrator to 135°F and turn it on. If your dehydrator has a built-in timer, set it for 7 hours. For models without a timer, set a separate timer.

3. At the 7-hour mark, check the rice and beans. The vegetables should be firm and should not feel moist. If necessary, continue to dry the vegetables for another 1 to 2 hours. The rice will dry more quickly than the vegetables; remove the rice when it is dry and hard to the touch.

## To Store

Measure the total amount of beans and rice separately. Divide both the beans and rice into four portions and place one portion of beans and one portion of rice in each of 4 boil-in bags. Label and date the bags. Store for up to 9 months.

## To Rehydrate

Add 1 cup of boiling water to the bag. Mix it well, cover, and let it sit about 15 minutes. Stir the rice and beans again before eating.

**NUTRITIONAL INFORMATION (PER SERVING):** 520 calories, 9g fat, 89g carb, 21g protein, 1150mg sodium (48% DV).

# RED CURRY VEGETABLE STIR-FRY

**GLUTEN FREE** · **NUT FREE FRIENDLY** · **SOY FREE** · **VEGAN**

**PREP TIME:** 15 MINUTES  **COOK TIME:** 20 MINUTES

**DEHYDRATION TIME:** 9 TO 11 HOURS  **REHYDRATION TIME:** 15 MINUTES

**WATER NEEDED FOR REHYDRATION (PER SERVING):** ⅔ CUP

**SERVES:** 4

1½ cups basmati or jasmine white rice

1 cup green beans, cut into 2-inch lengths

4 teaspoons oil, divided

1 teaspoon crushed ginger root

1 garlic clove, minced

2 tablespoons red curry paste

2 (13.5-ounce) cans light coconut milk (see ingredient tip)

1 teaspoon toasted sesame oil

½ teaspoon salt

1 tablespoon lime juice

1 small onion, thinly sliced

1 cup thinly sliced cremini mushrooms

1 medium carrot, cut into ⅛-inch rounds

½ medium red bell pepper, thinly sliced

¼ cup roughly chopped fresh cilantro

*continued*

*This dish doesn't have heat, but it is rich in flavor. If you are a heat-seeking soul, you might add a dash of sriracha to your stir-fry when cooking the sauce. Feel free to substitute your favorite stir-fry veggie for any of the listed vegetables.*

## To Prepare

1. Cook the rice according to the package directions, fluff it with a fork, and set it aside.

2. Heat a small saucepan over high heat and pour in 2 cups of water. Bring the water to a boil and add the green beans. Blanch for 1 minute, then remove the pan from the heat. Drain the beans then run cold water over them until they are at room temperature. Drain the beans again and set them aside.

**To pack for trail**
½ cup roasted peanuts or
cashews (optional)

3. Pour 2 teaspoons of oil in a large skillet over medium heat. Add the ginger and garlic and sauté for 30 seconds, stirring, until they are fragrant. Add the curry paste and cook for 1 minute longer. Add the coconut milk, sesame oil, salt, and lime juice. Bring to a simmer and cook for 5 minutes. Remove the skillet from the heat and pour the sauce into a medium bowl. Set the bowl aside.

4. Return the skillet to medium-high heat. Add the remaining 2 teaspoons of oil. When the oil is shimmering but not smoking, add the onions and cook, stirring, for 1 minute. Add the mushrooms, stir to mix, and cook without stirring for 1 minute. Add the carrots and bell pepper and cook for an additional minute. Add the green beans to the skillet.

5. Return the curry sauce to the skillet and bring it to a simmer. Lower the heat to medium and simmer gently for 2 to 3 minutes. Remove the stir-fry from the heat and stir in the cilantro.

CONTINUED ➤

**To Dehydrate**

1. Spread the stir-fry out on dehydrator trays fitted with a solid plastic insert, making sure that the sauce is evenly distributed among the trays. Place the rice on separate trays.

2. Place the trays in the dehydrator. Set the dehydrator to 135°F and turn it on. If your dehydrator has a built-in timer, set it for 9 hours. For models without a timer, set a separate timer.

3. At the 9-hour mark, check the stir-fry. The vegetables should be firm and should not feel moist. If necessary, continue to dry the stir-fry for another 1 to 2 hours. Rice dries more quickly than vegetables; remove the rice when it is dry and hard to the touch.

**To Store**

Measure the total amounts of the stir-fry and rice separately. Divide both the stir-fry and rice into four portions and place one portion of stir-fry and one portion of rice in each of four boil-in bags. Label and date the bags. Store for up to 2 months (the high fat content of the coconut milk, even when using light coconut milk, shortens the storage time of this meal). If you want to include the peanuts or cashews, divide them into four portions and place each portion in a small zip-sealed bag; sprinkle the contents of one bag on top of the stir-fry once it is rehydrated.

**To Rehydrate**

Add ⅔ cup of boiling water to the bag. Mix it well, cover, and let it sit for about 15 minutes. Stir the stir-fry again before eating.

**NUTRITIONAL INFORMATION (PER SERVING)**: 450 calories, 19g fat, 63g carb, 6g protein, 560mg sodium (23% DV).

## Ingredient Tip

Do not use regular coconut milk in this recipe, as the higher fat content makes it very difficult for the sauce to dehydrate.

CHAPTER EIGHT

# SNACKS AND DESSERTS

On the trail, snacks are huge! They get you through the day, especially those long-mile days where the path seems to go on forever. Plan to carry a few different snacks for a shorter trip and several kinds for longer trips so the selection won't bore you. Augment the recipes in this section with handfuls of savory nuts, dried fruits, and of course, chocolate. And speaking of chocolate, save some room for dessert! Nothing beats some comfort food at the end of the day, and the desserts in this chapter are easy to make—and even easier to eat.

# CRISPY CHICKPEAS

**DAIRY FREE** · **GLUTEN FREE** · **NUT FREE** · **SOY FREE** · **SUGAR FREE** · **VEGAN**

**PREP TIME:** 10 MINUTES **DEHYDRATION TIME:** 5 TO 7 HOURS

**SERVES:** 8

2 (28-ounce) cans chickpeas, rinsed and drained well

4 teaspoons olive oil

2 teaspoons ground cumin

½ teaspoon salt

½ teaspoon freshly ground black pepper

¼ teaspoon cayenne pepper

*These chickpeas are a fun snack to pop in your mouth on the trail, and they pack a surprising protein punch with 10 grams per serving. Vary the spices used in this recipe or try your favorite seasoning salt instead.*

### To Prepare

Put the chickpeas in a medium bowl and toss with the oil to coat. Add the cumin, salt, pepper, and cayenne and mix well to combine.

### To Dehydrate

1. Spread the chickpeas out evenly on the dehydrator trays.
2. Place the trays in the dehydrator. Set the dehydrator to 135°F and turn it on. If your dehydrator has a built-in timer, set it for 5 hours. For models without a timer, set a separate timer.
3. At the 5-hour mark, check the chickpeas. They should be firm and should not feel moist. If necessary, continue to dry the chickpeas for another 1 to 2 hours.

CONTINUED >

**To Store**

Measure the total amount of chickpeas, divide them into eight portions, and place each portion in a zip-sealed bag. Label and date the bags. Store for up to 9 months.

**NUTRITIONAL INFORMATION (PER SERVING):** 260 calories, 4.5g fat, 45 carb, 10g protein, 740mg sodium (31% DV).

# SAVORY BROCCOLI BITES

**DAIRY FREE** · **GLUTEN FREE** · **NUT FREE** · **SOY FREE** · **SUGAR FREE** · **VEGAN**

**PREP TIME:** 15 MINUTES   **COOK TIME:** 1 MINUTE   **DEHYDRATION TIME:** 6 TO 8 HOURS

**SERVES:** 4

2 large heads broccoli, cut into 1-inch florets

2 tablespoons olive oil

1 teaspoon seasoning salt

2 tablespoons hemp hearts (optional)

*These crispy snacks don't need to be rehydrated. They make a great savory snack for the trail, and there are many topping choices for the broccoli. The hemp hearts are one protein-rich option.*

**To Prepare**

1. In a medium pot over high heat, bring plenty of water to a boil. Add the broccoli to the pot and blanch it for 1 minute, then drain the broccoli and run it under ice-cold water to stop further cooking. Drain the broccoli well.

2. Put the broccoli in a medium bowl, add the oil, and toss it well. Add the salt and hemp hearts (if using), and toss again to combine.

**To Dehydrate**

1. Spread the broccoli out evenly on the dehydrator trays.

2. Place the trays in the dehydrator. Set the dehydrator to 140°F and turn it on. If your dehydrator has a built-in timer, set it for 6 hours. For models without a timer, set a separate timer.

CONTINUED >

3. At the 6-hour mark, check the broccoli. You'll know it's done when it feels firm and a bit crispy rather than moist. If necessary, continue to dry the broccoli for another 1 to 2 hours.

**To Store**

Measure the total amount of broccoli, divide it into four portions, and place each portion in a zip-sealed bag. Label and date the bags. Store for up to 9 months.

**NUTRITIONAL INFORMATION (PER SERVING)**: 190 calories, 10g fat, 21g carb, 10g protein, 290mg sodium (12% DV).

## Ingredient Tip

Use your favorite seasoning salt or explore the spice section at your grocery store for a new flavor. Nutritional yeast is a great way to add a cheesy flavor to this snack.

# VEGETABLE BEAN SALSA (COLD SOAK)

**DAIRY FREE** · **GLUTEN FREE** · **NUT FREE** · **SOY FREE** · **SUGAR FREE** · **VEGAN**

**PREP TIME:** 25 MINUTES  **DEHYDRATION TIME:** 6 TO 8 HOURS  **REHYDRATION TIME:** 15 MINUTES

**WATER NEEDED FOR REHYDRATION (PER SERVING):** ¼ CUP

**SERVES:** 4

1 large onion, cut into ¼-inch dice

6 Roma tomatoes, seeded and cut into ¼-inch dice

¾ cup finely chopped baby carrots

½ cup canned black beans, rinsed well and drained

2 jalapeño peppers, seeded and minced

⅛ serrano pepper, seeded and minced (optional)

½ cup packed fresh cilantro leaves, chopped

2 garlic cloves, minced

Juice of 1 lime

½ teaspoon salt

*This salsa provides a bright, fresh flavor when you are in the backcountry. Corn doesn't always rehydrate well with a cold soak, so in this recipe they have been swapped out for some baby carrots to provide a bit of sweetness.*

**To Prepare**

Mix all the ingredients together in a medium bowl. Check the seasoning and adjust to your taste.

**To Dehydrate**

1. Spread the salsa out evenly on the dehydrator trays fitted with a solid plastic tray insert.
2. Place the trays in the dehydrator. Set the dehydrator to 135°F and turn it on. If your dehydrator has a built-in timer, set it for 6 hours. For models without a timer, set a separate timer.
3. At the 6-hour mark, check the salsa. The vegetables should be firm and should not feel moist. If necessary, continue to dry the vegetables for another 1 to 2 hours.

CONTINUED ›

**To Store**

Measure the total amount of salsa, divide it into four portions, and place each portion in a zip-sealed bag. Label and date the bags. Store for up to 1 year.

**To Rehydrate**

Add ¼ cup of cool water to the bag. Mix it well, cover, and let it sit for about 15 minutes. Stir the salsa again before eating.

**NUTRITIONAL INFORMATION (PER SERVING)**: 80 calories, 0g fat, 18g carb, 4g protein, 430mg sodium (18% DV).

**Tip**
Pack some tortilla chips or carrots and celery to dip on your first day out on the trail.

# HUMMUS

**DAIRY FREE** • **GLUTEN FREE** • **NUT FREE** • **SOY FREE** • **SUGAR FREE** • **VEGAN**

**PREP TIME:** 20 MINUTES  **DEHYDRATION TIME:** 4 TO 6 HOURS  **REHYDRATION TIME:** 10 MINUTES
**WATER NEEDED FOR REHYDRATION (PER SERVING):** ¼ CUP
**SERVES:** 4

2 (15-ounce) cans chickpeas, rinsed and drained

⅓ cup water

4 tablespoons freshly squeezed lemon juice

2 tablespoons tahini

2 tablespoons olive oil

1 teaspoon minced garlic

½ teaspoon salt

## Optional Add-Ins

Add one of the following options, if desired.

⅔ cup roughly chopped Kalamata olives

½ cup roughly chopped sun-dried tomatoes (if using tomatoes packed in oil, reduce the olive oil by 1 teaspoon)

⅔ cup roughly chopped roasted red peppers (if using, reduce the water in the hummus by 1 tablespoon)

*Hummus makes a great trail snack and can be used as the foundation for a variety of wrap fillings. Here is a base recipe as well as a few ideas for switching up the flavor of the hummus.*

## To Prepare

Combine all the ingredients (including an add-in, if using) in a food processor or blender and purée for 2 minutes, stopping to scrape down the sides as needed. The longer processing time is necessary to create a creamy texture. Taste the hummus and adjust the seasonings, keeping in mind that as the hummus sits, the flavors will meld and the garlic will become a bit stronger.

## To Dehydrate

1. Spread the hummus out evenly on the dehydrator trays fitted with a solid plastic tray insert.

CONTINUED ➤

2. Place the trays in the dehydrator. Set the dehydrator to 135°F and turn it on. If your dehydrator has a built-in timer, set it for 4 hours. For models without a timer, set a separate timer.

3. At the 4-hour mark, check the hummus. It will be crackled and a bit dusty when dry. If necessary, continue to dry the hummus for another 1 to 2 hours.

### To Store

Measure the total amount of hummus, divide it into four portions, and place each portion in a zip-sealed bag. Label and date the bags. Store for up to 9 months.

### To Rehydrate

Add ¼ cup of cool water to the bag. Mix it well, cover, and let it sit for about 10 minutes. Stir the hummus again before eating.

**NUTRITIONAL INFORMATION (PER SERVING OF PLAIN HUMMUS)**: 320 calories, 9g fat, 51g carb, 12g protein, 930mg sodium (39% DV).

# SPINACH ARTICHOKE DIP (COLD SOAK)

**DAIRY FREE · GLUTEN FREE · SOY FREE · SUGAR FREE · VEGAN**

**PREP TIME:** 20 MINUTES **SOAKING TIME:** 1 TO 12 HOURS
**DEHYDRATION TIME:** 7 TO 9 HOURS **REHYDRATION TIME:** 5 MINUTES
**WATER NEEDED FOR REHYDRATION (PER SERVING):** ¼ CUP

**SERVES:** 4

1 cup raw cashews

½ cup water

2 tablespoons nutritional yeast

1 tablespoon olive oil

1 tablespoon freshly squeezed lemon juice

1 garlic clove, minced

¼ teaspoon salt

⅛ teaspoon freshly ground black pepper

6 ounces fresh spinach, roughly chopped

1 (14-ounce) can artichoke hearts in water, drained and roughly chopped

*This vibrantly colored dip has all the flavor of a traditional spinach artichoke dip, but with healthier ingredients. Use as a dip for chips, as a spread, or just eat it by the spoonful!*

## To Prepare

1. Soak the cashews in 1 cup of water, uncovered, for up to 12 hours. The longer the cashews are soaked, the creamier the sauce will be. Drain the and rinse cashews, then place them in a blender with ½ cup of fresh water. Do not reuse the soaking water. Blend until the mixture is smooth, adding more water by the tablespoon, if needed.

2. Add the nutritional yeast, oil, lemon juice, garlic, salt, and pepper to the blender and purée until well mixed.

3. Add the spinach and artichoke hearts and blend in pulses until just combined with the cashew mixture, scraping down the sides of the blender with a spatula as needed.

CONTINUED >

**To Dehydrate**

1. Spread the dip out evenly on the dehydrator trays fitted with a solid plastic tray insert.
2. Place the trays in the dehydrator. Set the dehydrator to 135°F and turn it on. If your dehydrator has a built-in timer, set it for 7 hours. For models without a timer, set a separate timer.
3. At the 7-hour mark, check the dip. It should be dry and should not feel moist. If necessary, continue to dry the dip for another 1 to 2 hours.

**To Store**

Measure the total amount of dip, divide it into four portions, and place each portion in a zip-sealed bag. Label and date the bags. Store for up to 9 months.

**To Rehydrate**

Add ¼ cup of cool water to the bag. Mix it well, cover, and let it sit for about 5 minutes. Stir the dip again before eating.

**NUTRITIONAL INFORMATION (PER SERVING):** 250 calories, 18 fat, 17g carb, 10g protein, 360mg sodium (15% DV).

# COCONUT RICE PUDDING WITH GOLDEN RAISINS

**GLUTEN FREE · NUT FREE · SOY FREE**

**PREP TIME:** 15 MINUTES  **COOK TIME:** 45 MINUTES

**DEHYDRATION TIME:** 7 TO 9 HOURS  **REHYDRATION TIME:** 15 MINUTES

**WATER NEEDED FOR REHYDRATION (PER SERVING):** ⅓ CUP

**SERVES:** 4

½ cup jasmine rice

½ cup light coconut milk

1½ cups whole milk

¼ cup golden raisins

1 tablespoon agave

½ teaspoon vanilla extract

¼ teaspoon ground cinnamon

⅛ teaspoon salt

½ cup unsweetened coconut chips

*The ultimate in comfort food, this creamy rice pudding is topped with crunchy toasted coconut chips. What a great way to end the day!*

## To Prepare

1. Preheat the oven to 250°F.

2. Place the rice, coconut milk, whole milk, raisins, agave, vanilla, cinnamon, and salt in a medium pot over medium-high heat and stir to combine. Bring the mixture to a boil, then immediately reduce the heat and cook at a low simmer, uncovered and stirring it frequently, for 40 to 45 minutes until the rice is creamy and the milk has thickened considerably.

3. While the rice is cooking, spread the coconut chips on a baking sheet and toast for 9 to 11 minutes until lightly golden brown. Set the coconut aside.

CONTINUED ⟩

### To Dehydrate

1. Once the pudding has cooled until lukewarm, spread the pudding out evenly on the dehydrator trays fitted with a solid plastic tray insert.
2. Place the trays in the dehydrator. Set the dehydrator to 135°F and turn it on. If your dehydrator has a built-in timer, set it for 7 hours. For models without a timer, set a separate timer.
3. At the 7-hour mark, check the pudding. The rice should be firm and the pudding dry, not moist. If necessary, continue to dry the pudding for another 1 to 2 hours.

### To Store

Measure the total amount of pudding, divide it into four portions, and place each portion in a boil-in bag. Divide the coconut chips equally into four small zip-sealed bags and insert one bag into each pudding bag. Label and date the bags. Store for up to 6 months.

### To Rehydrate

Remove the bag of coconut chips from the pudding bag. Add ⅓ cup of boiling water to the pudding bag. Mix it well, cover, and let it sit for about 15 minutes. Stir it again and sprinkle with the toasted coconut chips before eating.

**NUTRITIONAL INFORMATION (PER SERVING):** 430 calories, 22g fat, 52g carb, 4g protein, 180mg sodium (8% DV).

# BERRY CRISP

**DAIRY FREE · GLUTEN FREE · VEGAN**

**PREP TIME:** 25 MINUTES  **COOK TIME:** 30 MINUTES
**DEHYDRATION TIME:** 8 TO 10 HOURS  **REHYDRATION TIME:** 15 MINUTES
**WATER NEEDED FOR REHYDRATION (PER SERVING):** ⅓ CUP

**SERVES:** 4

Olive oil cooking spray

2 cups blueberries, fresh or frozen (thaw if frozen)

2 cups blackberries, fresh or frozen (thaw if frozen)

6 tablespoons almond flour, divided

1 cup gluten-free rolled oats (or regular oats if you tolerate gluten)

½ cup sliced almonds

⅛ teaspoon salt

2 tablespoons coconut oil

2 tablespoons agave

½ teaspoon vanilla extract

*This recipe uses a combination of blueberries and blackberries, but feel free to substitute either or both with your favorite berry.*

## To Prepare

1. Preheat the oven to 350°F and spray a square glass baking dish with cooking spray. Place the berries and any accumulated juices (if thawed from frozen) in the baking dish and add 2 tablespoons of almond flour. Mix to distribute the flour thoroughly.

2. In a small bowl, mix together the oats, the remaining 4 tablespoons of almond flour, the almonds, and salt. Add the coconut oil, agave, and vanilla and stir to combine thoroughly.

3. Sprinkle the oat topping evenly over the berries until the berries are mostly covered, to the edge of the baking dish. You should be able to see a small number of berries peeking through. Make sure that the oats don't accumulate in a thick layer or they will not crisp. You may have a couple of tablespoons of oat topping left over, which you can discard.

CONTINUED ➤

4. Bake the crisp for 25 to 30 minutes or until the topping is crisp and lightly golden and the berries are bubbling up over the topping. If the topping browns before the berries are bubbling, cover the baking dish tightly with aluminum foil and cook for another 5 minutes.

5. Allow the crisp to cool to room temperature, then use your fingers or a spoon to scrape the topping from the crisp. Place the topping in a small bowl. The goal is to get most of the topping off the berries, but it's not necessary to get all of it. Once you've removed the majority of the topping, mix the berries with a spoon to redistribute any leftover topping.

**To Dehydrate**

1. Spread the berry crisp thinly, flattening any fat berries, on the dehydrator trays fitted with a solid plastic insert. Spread the topping out evenly on a separate tray.

2. Place the trays in the dehydrator. Set the dehydrator to 145°F and turn it on. If your dehydrator has a built-in timer, set it for 8 hours. For models without a timer, set a separate timer.

3. At the 8-hour mark, check the crisp. The berries should be able to bend but not break, and come off the dehydrator tray insert in sheets, similar to fruit leather. If necessary, continue to dry the crisp for another 1 to 2 hours. The topping will dry more quickly than the berry portion of the crisp; remove the topping when it is dry and firm to the touch.

### To Store

Measure the total amount of crisp and topping separately. Divide each into four portions. Place each portion of crisp in a boil-in bag. Place each portion of topping in a small, zip-sealed bag. Place one topping bag inside each crisp bag. Label and date the bags. Store for up to 1 year.

### To Rehydrate

Remove the topping bag then add ⅓ cup of boiling water to the crisp bag. Mix it well, cover, and let it sit for about 15 minutes. Stir the crisp again and sprinkle with the topping, before eating.

**NUTRITIONAL INFORMATION (PER SERVING):** 450 calories, 20g fat, 61g carb, 11g protein, 80mg sodium (3% DV).

## Preparation Tip

Although it may seem counterintuitive to put the topping on the berries to cook, only to scrape it back off again when the crisp is done, I recommend this method because the topping absorbs some of the lovely berry juices during the baking process, and that enhances the overall flavor of the dish.

# BREAD PUDDING WITH CHERRIES AND CHOCOLATE

**MEAT FREE • NUT FREE • SOY FREE**

**PREP TIME:** 30 MINUTES  **SOAKING TIME:** 4 TO 12 HOURS (OPTIONAL)  **COOK TIME:** 50 MINUTES
**DEHYDRATION TIME:** 8 TO 10 HOURS  **REHYDRATION TIME:** 15 MINUTES
**WATER NEEDED FOR REHYDRATION (PER SERVING):** ¼ CUP

**SERVES:** 8

½ cup dried cherries (see page 31 for instructions on drying apples and pears)

1 ounce bourbon (optional)

3 eggs

½ cup sugar

1½ cups whole milk

½ cup half and half or heavy cream

½ teaspoon vanilla extract

¼ teaspoon ground cinnamon

¼ teaspoon salt

Butter, softened, to grease the baking dish

6 cups torn stale challah or brioche bread (2-inch-square pieces)

1 (2-ounce) bar baking chocolate, semi or bittersweet, roughly chopped

*Bread pudding in the backcountry? You bet. This is a wonderfully decadent way to reward yourself after a grueling day on the trail, or maybe just to celebrate being outside.*

There are two options to make the challah or brioche bread stale. The first is to place the bread pieces on a baking sheet and bake them in the oven on the lowest temperature. Leave the bread in the oven for 10 to 15 minutes or until the bread surface is dry. Do not allow the bread to toast. Alternatively, place the bread pieces on a baking sheet, cover with a clean dish towel, and leave out overnight.

**To Prepare**

1. If using bourbon, soak the cherries in the bourbon in a small bowl for at least 4 hours and up to overnight.

2. Whisk the eggs in a large bowl. Add the sugar in a thin stream, whisking until all the sugar is incorporated. Add the milk and half and half and mix well. Add the vanilla, cinnamon, and salt.

3. Grease a square baking dish with a light layer of butter. Put the bread in the dish and pour the egg mixture over the bread. Toss gently so that all the bread is soaked. Let the bread mix sit for 20 minutes.

4. Preheat the oven to 350°F.

5. Add the cherries and chocolate to the bread, tossing gently to combine.

6. Bake for 45 to 50 minutes, or until the surface is golden and crusty and the custard is just set.

**To Dehydrate**

1. Allow the bread pudding to cool completely. Slice the pudding into ¼-inch-thick slices and lay them on the dehydrator trays fitted with a solid plastic tray insert. If the pudding is too difficult to cut thinly, try chilling it in the freezer for about 20 minutes before cutting.

2. Place the trays in the dehydrator. Set the dehydrator to 145°F and turn it on. If your dehydrator has a built-in timer, set it for 8 hours. For models without a timer, set a separate timer.

CONTINUED ➤

3. At the 8-hour mark, check the bread pudding. It should be firm and should not feel moist. If necessary, continue to dry the pudding for another 1 to 2 hours.

**To Store**

Measure the total amount of pudding, divide it into four portions, and place each portion in a boil-in bag. Label and date the bags. Store for up to 3 months.

**To Rehydrate**

Add ¼ cup of boiling water to the bag. Mix it well, cover, and let it sit for about 15 minutes. Stir the pudding again before eating.

**NUTRITIONAL INFORMATION (PER SERVING)**: 300 calories, 10g fat, 43g carb, 8g protein, 250mg sodium (10% DV).

## Rehydration Tip

The chocolate maintains its form during the dehydration process but will melt during rehydration. It still imparts a great chocolatey flavor, but if you prefer, you can leave the chocolate out until the pudding is rehydrated, then sprinkle it on top.

# SAMPLE MEAL PLAN

Time for the weekend! The workweek is done, and you are headed out on the trail for a couple nights. What are you going to pack for your meals?

## Friday

Let's start with Friday afternoon. Depending on what time you can hit the road, you probably only need a snack and some dinner. Pack a portion of your favorite *Hummus* (page 147) and some baby carrots or a tortilla for a satisfying late-afternoon snack.

For dinner, try some *Cilantro Pesto Pasta with Veggies* (page 125). This vibrantly colored pasta includes a bunch of veggies to augment your meal.

## Saturday

Start your day with a bowl of *Cinnamon Apple Hazelnut Oatmeal* (page 71) and a *Power Shake* (page 89).

For a mid-morning snack, take a handful of dried fruits and nuts.

At lunchtime, find a picturesque place to stop and enjoy some *Lemony Lentil Salad* (page 97).

Dinnertime is for relaxing. Have a bowl of *Spicy Sweet Potato and Chorizo Stew* (page 106) and treat yourself with *Bread Pudding with Cherries and Chocolate* (page 156).

## Sunday

The *Salmon and Roasted Sweet Potato Hash* (page 79) is a perfect Sunday morning breakfast. The dish is hearty and filling but won't load you down for the hike out.

Pack some more hummus for a mid-morning snack, along with a tortilla to roll up with the hummus.

# MEASUREMENT CONVERSIONS

| | US STANDARD | US STANDARD (OUNCES) | METRIC (APPROXIMATE) |
|---|---|---|---|
| **VOLUME EQUIVALENTS (LIQUID)** | 2 tablespoons | 1 fl. oz. | 30 mL |
| | ¼ cup | 2 fl. oz. | 60 mL |
| | ½ cup | 4 fl. oz. | 120 mL |
| | 1 cup | 8 fl. oz. | 240 mL |
| | 1½ cups | 12 fl. oz. | 355 mL |
| | 2 cups or 1 pint | 16 fl. oz. | 475 mL |
| | 4 cups or 1 quart | 32 fl. oz. | 1 L |
| | 1 gallon | 128 fl. oz. | 4 L |
| **VOLUME EQUIVALENTS (DRY)** | ⅛ teaspoon | | 0.5 mL |
| | ¼ teaspoon | | 1 mL |
| | ½ teaspoon | | 2 mL |
| | ¾ teaspoon | | 4 mL |
| | 1 teaspoon | | 5 mL |
| | 1 tablespoon | | 15 mL |
| | ¼ cup | | 59 mL |
| | ⅓ cup | | 79 mL |
| | ½ cup | | 118 mL |
| | ⅔ cup | | 156 mL |
| | ¾ cup | | 177 mL |
| | 1 cup | | 235 mL |
| | 2 cups or 1 pint | | 475 mL |
| | 3 cups | | 700 mL |
| | 4 cups or 1 quart | | 1 L |
| | ½ gallon | | 2 L |
| | 1 gallon | | 4 L |
| **WEIGHT EQUIVALENTS** | ½ ounce | | 15 g |
| | 1 ounce | | 30 g |
| | 2 ounces | | 60 g |
| | 4 ounces | | 115 g |
| | 8 ounces | | 225 g |
| | 12 ounces | | 340 g |
| | 16 ounces or 1 pound | | 455 g |

CONTINUED ≫

| | FAHRENHEIT (F) | CELSIUS (C) (APPROXIMATE) |
|---|---|---|
| **OVEN TEMPERATURES** | 170°F | 77°C |
| | 250°F | 120°C |
| | 300°F | 150°C |
| | 325°F | 180°C |
| | 375°F | 190°C |
| | 400°F | 200°C |
| | 425°F | 220°C |
| | 450°F | 230°C |

# INDEX

# ACKNOWLEDGMENTS

Sue, Sharon, Ann, and Bob: Thank you for tasting and testing recipes and volunteering your time and opinions when I needed them the most.

Grant, Mark, Elayna, and Libby, my staff at Food for the Sole: Thank you for all the support, especially your coverage in the kitchen while I was buried in the writing of this book, and for being willing to answer all my random questions.

Henry, my son and business partner: I couldn't have done this without you, and truly, I wouldn't want to. You make this whole adventure worthwhile.

# ABOUT THE AUTHOR

 Julie Mosier has always made food one of the most significant parts of her life, from cooking and catering both professionally and for fun, to feeding gatherings of family and friends at every opportunity. After 20 years spent working in higher education, Julie wanted to fulfill a lifelong goal of owning a business. In partnership with her son, she launched Food for the Sole, which makes dehydrated backpacking meals. Based in Bend, Oregon, Julie and her son lead a small team of outdoor-oriented employees in creating small-batch meals with a focus on fresh-tasting vegetables. They believe that people should be able to eat well anytime, anyplace, whether in the backcountry or at home.

Printed in the USA
CPSIA information can be obtained
at www.ICGtesting.com
CBHW052320280424
7402CB00012B/15